THE ULTIMATE GUIDE TO
GREAT SEX

THE ULTIMATE GUIDE TO
GREAT SEX

Paula Hall

GRAMERCY BOOKS
NEW YORK

This 2005 edition is published by Gramercy Books, an imprint of Random House Value Publishing, a division of Random House, Inc., New York, by arrangement with Kandour Ltd, London.

Gramercy is a registered trademark and the colophon is a trademark of Random House, Inc.

Random House
New York • Toronto • London • Sydney • Auckland
www.randomhouse.com

Author: Paula Hall
Managing editor: Jenny Ross
Cover design: George Georgiou
Page layout: Esme Bradbury
Illustrations: Diana Friedrich and Mervyn Diese
Editorial & design management: Metro Media

Photography: photos.com, Loving-angles.com™ (p57 (top), 108, 109-113),
Esme Bradbury (p121, 129, 124-125, 131 (top)), Alex Treacher (p114, 126, 130 (top), 132, 134),
Rex Features (p100, 103, 106, (Iris Honold), 107 (Image Source), 128 (Shilo/Israel Sun)),
photolibrary.com (p101, 108 (bottom), 151, 152), *The Hot Spot* magazine (p121)

With thanks to: Jonathan Jackson, Loving-angles (Angles Global Ltd)®
and Paul Gorman

Printed and bound in India

A catalog record for this title is available from the Library of Congress.

ISBN 0-517-22678-2

10 9 8 7 6 5 4 3 2 1

About the author

Paula Hall is a sexual & relationship psychotherapist who has been working with couples and individuals who want to improve their sex lives for over 10 years. She has been consulted by literally hundreds of people from all walks of life.

Paula works for Relate, the British marriage guidance counseling organization, and also maintains a private practice. She has UKCP registration and is BASRT accredited. She also offers an internet-based service at www.sextherapyonline.org.

She is the author of the BBC website section on sex and couples and is a consultant for BBC Science and BBC Documentaries, providing advice and analysis on sex and relationships.

As an expert on relationships and sexuality, Paula Hall provides regular commentary in the national press and in women's magazines and has appeared on such British national radio and television shows, including *Richard & Judy*, BBC Radio 4's *Woman's Hour,* and the BBC Science series, *Dangerous Passions*.

Contents

THE ULTIMATE GUIDE TO
GREAT SEX

Sex is possibly life's most profound and fulfilling physical experience. As well as offering great satisfaction, sex unites two people as nothing else can. Sex is good for the health, increases longevity, builds positivity and self-esteem, and strengthens relationships. For many people, sex is the most intimate expression of love. It is the act that makes relationships unique and special.

Unfortunately, early experiences of sex can also be disappointing. Consequently, many people feel let down, even betrayed by the promises of sex. Some women say they would prefer to hug rather than make love, because sex does not offer the intimacy they expected. On the other hand, some men turn to pornography, frustrated that sex does not offer the excitement they have been promised. Many couples give up on ever achieving a great sex life and accept mediocre experiences as the norm.

We must not believe the myth that, because sex is natural, great sex comes naturally. Being in love doesn't mean that we know how to make love. Great sex takes time, effort, and, above all, commitment. Commitment to be loving, commitment to be open, and commitment to be adventurous.

This book has been written to help you and your partner enjoy great sex. It starts with advice on how to develop positive sexual confidence, exploring sexual attitudes and needs, and exposing unhelpful beliefs and preconceptions. It also provides inside information on becoming sexually fit and understanding how the male and the female body both respond to stimulation.

You will also learn how to create the conditions you need for great sex and how to put it all into action. There are sections on relationship intimacy and communication as well as guidance on giving an erotic massage.

Chapters five through nine cover masturbation, oral sex, intercourse, sex toys, erotica, sex games, fantasy, and tantric sex. We also discuss how sex changes in long-term relationships, during parenting, and as you age. Finally, there's a chapter on how to manage sexual difficulties if and when they occur. There's specific advice for dealing with problems of erection and ejaculation, painful intercourse and difficulty reaching orgasm, as well as problems with sexual desire.

The Ultimate Guide to Great Sex has been written from an able-bodied, heterosexual viewpoint though most of the information and advice applies to gay and lesbian lovers as well as to people with disabilities and their partners. I hope that whatever your sexual orientation or ability, you will find something helpful and inspiring in these pages.

Paula Hall
Author

It's all about you

Great sex starts with yourself. If you want to enjoy great sex, it's important for you to get to know your sexual self. You need to ensure you have positive sexual attitudes and feel comfortable and confident about your sexual needs. You should also try to develop a positive view of your physical self. Then you can look forward to a lifetime of great sex.

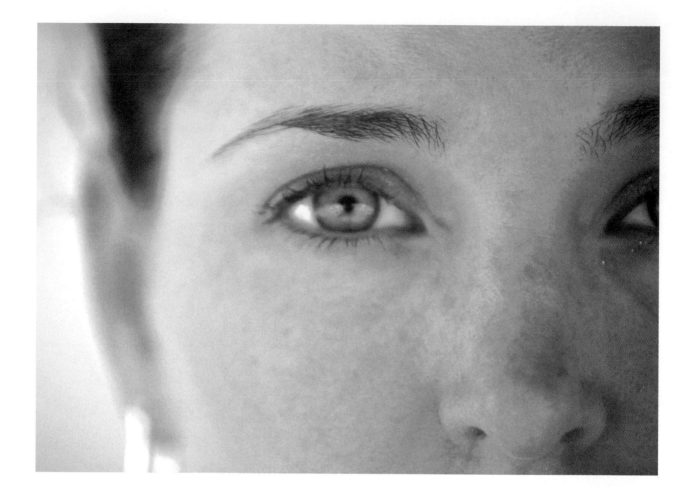

Sexual attitudes

Each of us has a unique view not only of our sexual selves but also of how sex should be. These views are formed in early childhood from the relationships and experiences we see around us and grow and develop as we mature. If the impact is negative then it is important that any issues are addressed.

Messages from childhood

From the moment you inquisitively put your hand down your underpants or panties, your parents' response influences how you view your sexuality. And so do the messages you pick up about nudity. Was it okay to run around naked? Or did "nice" girls and boys keep their private parts covered?

Then there's the interaction you saw between your parents. How often did you see them kiss? Did they ever giggle together or have an early night? And what happened if there was a sexy scene on television? Did the room go quiet or did dad make a sudden lunge for the remote?

Our parents are hugely influential in what they say—and in what they don't say. We learn whether or not sex is okay, natural, private, rude, or even disgusting—often before we've even reached puberty.

Messages from puberty

As your body begins to change, the puberty years can also be hugely influential. How did the rest of your family react to your sexual development? Was it celebrated or was it a time to dish out dire warnings on the dangers of sex? And how did you feel about your body?

If you're a woman, were you proud of your growing breasts? As a man, were you proud of your deepening voice and increasing body hair? Or did you feel self-conscious and embarrassed? When those early sexual urges kicked in, did it feel natural and healthy? Or were you left with feelings of doubt, anxiety, and shame?

IF YOU'VE HAD A TRAUMATIC SEXUAL EXPERIENCE

Unfortunately, sexual violence and abuse is far more common than many people think. If you've had an experience in your past that has left you feeling uncomfortable in any way, then please, please find someone to talk to about it. An experienced counselor can help you work through your feelings and reduce the impact it will have on your future. You can find details of advisory agencies at the back of this book.

Early sexual experiences

For some people, those early fumbles behind the schoolhouse left them with fond memories—but for others, they were awkward or even traumatic experiences. Our early sexual experiences should be a time of safe experimentation, but for some this is when fears and doubts about our attractiveness and performance are formed. Other people find they're left with unrealistic expectations of permanent passion and buzz.

Influence of religion and culture

Those of us who were brought up within a strict religious or cultural environment may also be affected by the sexual messages related to the various doctrines. You have to decide if you still agree with those views. And if so, do they have a positive or negative impact on your sexual relationships? If these are views you no longer hold, how do you feel about the change in your perspective?

It is perfectly possible to have a strong religious faith or cultural heritage and still have great sex. There may be some sexual practices that you choose not to engage in, but as long as you and your partner are both agreed you have a sound basis for sex to be great.

AN EXERCISE TO DO ALONE OR WITH YOUR PARTNER

Look at the list of words below and choose as many as you like to describe the following:

- **How you felt about sex when you were a child**
- **How you felt about sex when you were a teenager**
- **How you felt about your first sexual experience**

Exciting	Alarming	Warm
Erotic	Painful	Unifying
Intense	Boring	Memorable
Animal	Angry	Emotional
Gentle	Threatening	Magical
Energetic	Frightening	Silly
Thrilling	Reassuring	Tiring
Ecstatic	Happy	Annoying
Passionate	Satisfying	Pointless
Sordid	Cosy	Routine
Urgent	Intimate	Rude
Primitive	Romantic	Mundane
Disgusting	Fun	Generous
Embarrassing	Mystical	Uncomfortable
Loving	Relaxing	Depressing
Rude	Sensual	Sad
Immature	Friendly	

If you can, make some time to share this exercise with your partner and discuss anything new that you've learned.

A POSITIVE VIEW OF SEX

- Everyone has a right to be sexual.
- Sex is a healthy expression of intimacy.
- Sex can be physically rewarding.
- Sex can be fun and playful.
- Sex can be sensual and erotic.
- Sex can make you feel good about yourself and your partner.

Beliefs and myths

It seems to me that that the more we learn about sex, the more rigid our views become. And as we strive for a more fulfilling sex life, the higher we raise our expectations and the harder it is to meet them. Most of us have preconceptions about sex. Here are just a few myths for you to think about.

Sex should always be natural and spontaneous—planning or talking about it spoils it.

This particularly annoys me. Why should spontaneous sex be better? The vacation you've been planning and looking forward to for six months would be no better purely if it had been booked on the spur of the moment. In fact, it could well be worse! I'm not saying that an unexpected "quickie" can't be fantastic. But remember that planning builds anticipation. And anticipation builds arousal.

If two people *really* love each other then sex is automatically good.

Great sex is not a natural instinct. Like most things in life it has to be learned and practiced—and we all know that eventually practice makes perfect. Sex is no different, though practicing sex with someone special is great fun.

You don't need to tell a good lover what you like, they will know.

This is a variation on the myth above—it says that good lovers instinctively know what to do, that a good lover somehow knows how to tune in with their partner. Unless you're a mind-reader this is nonsense. Great lovers know that talking to their partner about sex not only improves their technique but also increases intimacy.

Men always want sex, and are always ready for it.

There are still a surprising number of men (and their partners) who expect the penis to respond like a well-oiled piece of machinery. Completely detached from the brain, it's meant to be ready at all times and with minimal stimulation. While it's true that men generally do have a higher sex drive than women, like their

female counterparts men also experience tiredness and stress. You can't separate sexual function from your brain and your feelings. All men have times when they're just not interested or not capable.

Having sex means having intercourse.

There is this myth that unless you're having intercourse, you're not really having sex, just foreplay. This is based on the belief that everything else, whether manual and oral stimulation or the rich and diverse variety of non-penetrative practices, should naturally lead to penetration. People who believe this are missing out on so much. Sex is about closeness, sensuality, pleasure, and touch—it starts when you feel sexy and stops when you don't.

Wanting sex shows how much you love each other.

Some people use sex as a way of showing affection. This means that if their partner isn't in the mood, they feel unloved. Sex is a great way of becoming close to one another and showing how much you care for someone, but remember, it is only one way to express how you feel, not the only way.

Sexual liberation means trying everything.

This is simply untrue. Sexual tastes vary from individual to individual. There's no right or

If you are sexually confident— you are attractive

wrong way to enjoy great sex. If there are some things that just don't make you horny, don't do them. Sexual liberation means having the confidence to do what you want, when you want, and if you want.

Only young, fit, slim, beautiful and able-bodied people enjoy great sex.

Our TV screens and magazines hardly ever show anyone enjoying sex who is over 25 or has a less-than-perfect body. Good looks may be helpful for sexual attraction, but not for great sex. It doesn't matter how beautiful you are, if you're selfish, cruel, and sexually unresponsive, then no one is going to find you sexy. Anyone and everyone can have great sex. It doesn't matter how old you are, how big you are, how fit you are, or how symmetrical your body is. If you're sexually confident— you're attractive.

THE 6–2–2 RULE

I hate to write this, but you should bear in mind that sex won't be great every single time you have it.

In fact, one theory says that out of every 10 times you have sex, six times it'll be pretty good, twice it'll be absolutely fantastic—and twice you'll wish you hadn't bothered. Oh—and remember, if there's two of you, you can't guarantee your "fantastic" won't be their "wish I hadn't bothered."

Sexual needs

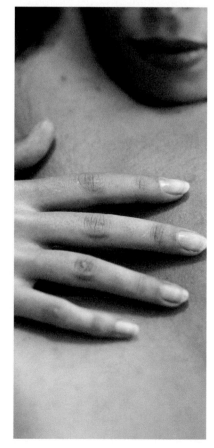

Great sex takes more than knowledge of the latest sexual techniques. Your lover could be the most skilled sexual virtuoso in the universe, but if sexual needs aren't being met, you're both wasting your time. It is important to consider your physical well-being and emotional and relationship needs.

We all have different sexual needs. To understand what you need to make sex satisfying and fulfilling you need to recognize and respect your physical and emotional desires.

Some of these sexual needs may be absolutely essential for you to be able to have a good time. Others might be things that you would prefer but can live without.

Your physical needs

When I talk about your physical needs, I'm not discussing the kind of stimulation you need to feel aroused or reach orgasm—that's covered in Chapter 5. Here I'm referring to your general physical wellbeing and also your physical environment. For example, most people need to feel reasonably relaxed and awake in order to enjoy sex. They also need to be in good health and not in too much pain or discomfort.

With regard to environment, think about what conditions you need. Do you need to be in a warm, comfortable room or is the back of the car okay? Do you prefer sex with the lights off or with subdued lighting? And what about privacy? Some couples need to be sure that they definitely won't be interrupted, while others find a little danger adds to the excitement.

Your emotional needs

If you are feeling anxious, sad, angry, or depressed—then sex is not going to be good. And it definitely won't be if you're scared of getting pregnant, scared of being caught, scared of ruining your reputation, or contracting a disease. For most people, feeling relaxed is an essential emotional need. There are a few who enjoy the extra adrenalin surge of a risky

Our sexual needs change and grow with us, because sex means different things at different times

encounter, but generally this is counterbalanced by the knowledge that any negative consequence can be managed. Another essential for most of us is to feel ready for sex. That means not being preoccupied

SEXUAL NEEDS

Before you start any sexual experience ask yourself the following questions:
1. Am I feeling relaxed and happy with myself?
2. Am I confident that my partner is happy and relaxed?
3. Can I readily accept any possible consequences of this encounter?
4. Does my partner have the same expectations as I do?
5. Am I physically comfortable?

with work or problems. There are some tips for getting in the mood in Chapter 3.

Your relationship needs

Our greatest sexual needs usually involve our partner. Feeling safe with our sexual partner means knowing that we're accepted. It means knowing that our body and our performance are not being judged. And knowing that our partner is enjoying the sexual experience as much as we are.

Our sexual needs change and grow, because sex means different things to us at different times, with different partners. Be ready to reassess your sexual needs on a regular basis and don't expect to have great sex if those basic needs aren't being met.

DISCOVERING YOUR SEXUAL NEEDS

Think back to two occasions when you had really great sex. Now remember two sexual experiences that were disappointing.

Comparing those good and bad sexual experiences, what was different? Think about the physical things that were different; for example, the place and time of day. Think also about the emotional factors. How relaxed were you? What else was going on in your life at that time? Finally, think about whether you felt differently toward your partner on those occasions. Now use that information to begin to build your personal list of sexual needs.

Feeling fit for sex

Research shows that regular exercise can boost your libido and enhance your sexual pleasure. Feeling happy about your body will make you more confident with your partner and increasing your fitness level will also give you more stamina and energy. Before starting any exercise regime always consult your doctor.

Getting physical

Regular exercise can improve the way you look and feel. In combination with a balanced diet, regular activity reduces stress and rejuvenates the body, filling you with renewed vigor, greater confidence, the glow of good health and, best of all, a better sex life.

Daily, moderately intense physical activity burns approximately 200 calories per day. This equates to about 30 minutes of activity, such as a two-mile brisk walk. During moderate-intensity activity, you should still be able to talk without panting in between your words.

If 30 minutes of exercise in one session isn't practical, then try separate 10-minute sessions.

It's possible to achieve this target by making fairly simple changes to your everyday routine, without having to join a gym.

Examples of everyday activities include:
• Walking up stairs instead of using elevators.
• Walking up moving escalators.
• Walking instead of driving for short journeys.
• Doing housework in "double-time."
• Fixing up your home, such as painting or mowing the lawn.

Your ability to maintain a physical activity such as jogging, racket sports, cycling, or swimming, is related to your aerobic fitness or stamina.

Generally speaking, the greater your stamina, the greater the health benefits. If you want to improve your stamina, it's important to start gently, increasing the frequency of activity before trying to exercise harder.

It's important to find an activity, or range of activities, that you enjoy. Not everyone sees exercise as fun, and doing something you find boring just because it's good for you is very difficult to sustain.

Getting sexy

Whether it's flexing your pelvic floor muscles (see overleaf) or toning your butt, there are certain exercises that will directly benefit your sex life.

Here are are three exercises that you can do at home:

Inner thigh squeeze

Your inner thigh muscles come in very handy during sex. Try this exercise to tone and strengthen muscles.
• Lie on floor, arms to side, stomach muscles zipped in toward your naval, knees bent.
• Place a pillow or folded towel between your knees.
• With your feet together, squeeze the pillow using your inner thighs, and tilting your hips an inch upward as you do so. Hold for a count of five. Repeat 15 times.
• Finish set off with 15 single repetitions, holding for a second each time.

Toning your butt

This will ensure you butt stays high and tight.
• Lie on your back, feet hip-width apart and knees bent with feet flat on the floor.
• Lift your hips toward the ceiling –do not lift yourself onto your shoulders, only a small lift. Squeeze knees in toward each other and out again.
• Lower the butt down one inch and up again. Squeeze. Continue to alternate, always pulling up the pelvic floor. Try for 10 alternations then rest. Next time, try and build up to more repetitions.

Seated chest opener

This is a great exercise for your posture. Standing tall and proud helps you feel more confident, as

Regular exercise will increase the blood flow to the genitals, priming your body for sex

well as adding inches to your chest.
• Sit in a comfortable cross-legged position.
• Place both hands about 6–12in behind you with your fingers facing toward you. Allow your body to lean back slightly.
• Open your chest by lifting your breastbone up toward the sky and allow your head to fall back slightly without straining.

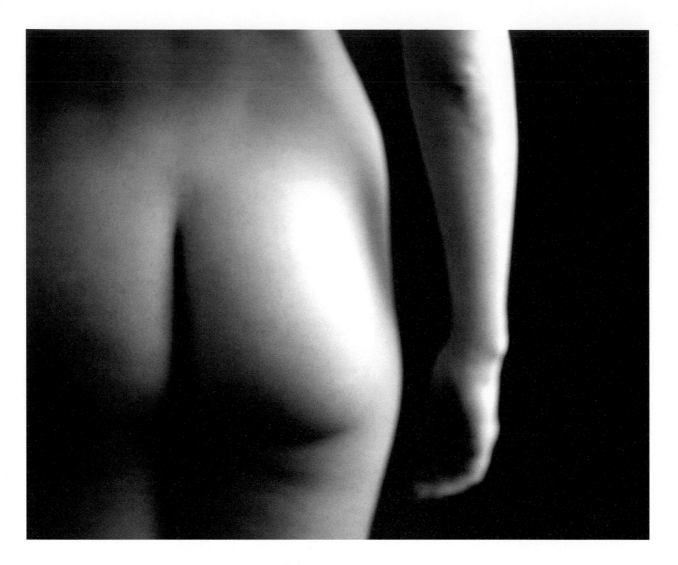

Regular exercise of the PC muscles has many health benefits for men and for women

Exercising your pelvic floor muscles

Time required: a few minutes every day.

To start, you need to be sure you have located your pelvic floor muscles. You can do this by stopping your flow of urine next time you go to the bathroom. The muscles you use to do this are your PC muscles.

Now, start by squeezing and releasing these muscles 15 times. Don't hold the contraction, just squeeze and release. Begin by doing one set of 15, twice a day.

Try to concentrate on squeezing only your pelvic floor muscles, not your stomach and thighs. It will become easier with practice. Do the exercises every day, gradually increasing the number until you can do 40 or 50 at a time. Build up slowly. When you are comfortable doing 40 or 50, you can vary the exercise by holding each contraction to the count of 3 before releasing. Again, build up slowly until you can achieve 40 or 50.

You can do these exercises anywhere and at any time. No one needs to know you are doing them. Practice sitting, standing, and lying down. Most importantly, find a time when you remember to do them every day. It may take up to six weeks for you to notice some of the benefits listed above, but you will feel them. This is an exercise that can help you get the most from your sexual activity, an exercise for life!

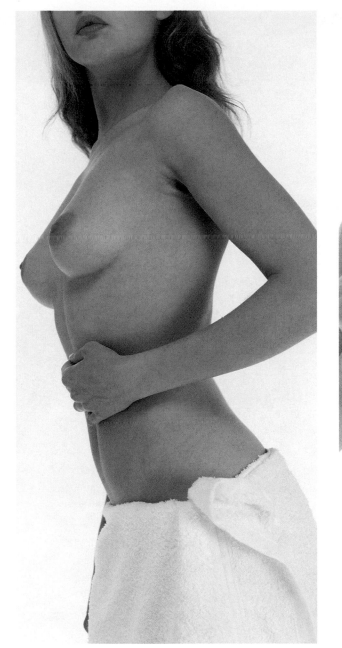

Benefits for women
- Improved blood circulation to the genital area which will assist sexual arousal.

- Greater feeling of control and confidence on vaginal penetration.

- Stronger and more pleasurable orgasms.

- Helps avoid urinary incontinence.

- Helps avoid vaginal prolapse.

- Increased sensation on vaginal penetration for both partners.

Benefits for men
- Stronger and more pleasurable orgasms.

- Improvement in the angle of erection.

- Improved blood circulation to the genital area which will assist sexual arousal and may assist erection.

- Avoidance of urinary incontinence.

- Greater feeling of control and confidence over ejaculation.

Body basics

What they never taught you in Sex Ed

Many of us can't remember anything about sex education at school, apart from the giggles of students and the embarrassment of the teacher. At best you'll have learned how to make babies—but you won't have learned how to make love. In this chapter, we tell you everything you need to know about how you and your partner's bodies respond to sexual stimulation.

Exploring yourself

Perhaps we shouldn't be surprised at how little we know about our physical responses to sex. Growing up, the average child learns the names of most but not all body parts. We will be encouraged as we recognize hands, feet, and belly, but genitals are not likely to get a mention.

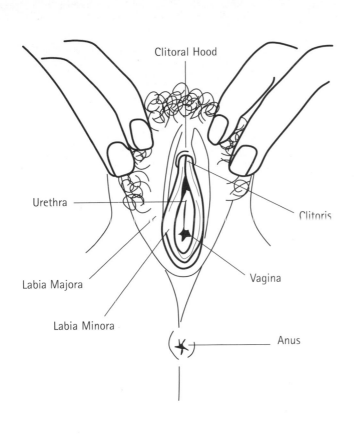

Clitoral Hood

Urethra

Clitoris

Labia Majora

Vagina

Labia Minora

Anus

Female genitalia

While little boys have the ability to have a good look and a play to find out about the most intimate parts of their physical make-up, young girls (unless they're double-jointed!) are unlikely to ever see exactly what lies between their legs without the help of a mirror. So not only are women's genitals a mystery to men, they are often a mystery to women too.

As you can see from the diagram above, the female genitalia is made up of the external lips (*labia majora*) and internal lips (*labia minora*). The outer lips mainly provide protection for the internal genitals and the internal lips. The place where the inner lips meet is the clitoris, the area most responsible for female sexual pleasure. The clitoris has more nerve endings per square inch than any other part of the body. As well as the head of the clitoris that is protected by the clitoral hood, the clitoris extends into the body cavity. Beneath the clitoris is the urethra, the opening where urine is passed out of the body. Beneath this is the vagina. In its unaroused state, the vaginal opening is small. The area between the vagina and the anus is called the perineum.

It's important to know that all women's genitals are different. In the same way as no two faces are the same, no two women have genitals that look the same. And in the same way as most of us will have one ear bigger than the other, the labia are rarely symmetrical. Many women can feel self-conscious about how their genitals look, but as more and more positive images are becoming available, this is hopefully becoming a thing of the past.

The clitoris has more nerve endings per square inch than any other part of the body

To the right, you will see the layout of the internal female sexual organs. This diagram should already be familiar, though it's generally used to discuss reproduction rather than sex. You can see one of the two ovaries where the egg is produced and the uterus where a child is developed if an egg is fertilized. The important thing to notice here is how the vaginal walls lie closely together when a woman is unaroused and the cervix and uterus are just above the vagina. The unaroused vagina is not designed for penetration. But when it is sexually excited, it's a different story altogether. The vagina is rich in nerve endings, but the vast majority of these are in the lower third around the entrance.

The other area of female anatomy that is often misunderstood is the G-spot. Some women say their G-spot is highly erogenous, while others find it uncomfortable to the touch. Some claim they don't have one at all. The early fetus has the potential to develop either male or female sex organs, depending on the presence of the Y chromosome. If you've got XX chromosomes you'll develop into a girl with a vagina, clitoris, and uterus. If you've got XY chromosomes you'll be a boy and those same cells will develop into a penis, testes, and prostate.

Now, remembering that both sexes have the same cells, scientists reckon that the G-spot develops from unused prostate tissue. If this is the case, it would account for the sensitivity and responsiveness (we know the male prostate is very sensitive). It would also account for the huge variation in size. Some tissue deposits are so small that they're unnoticeable.

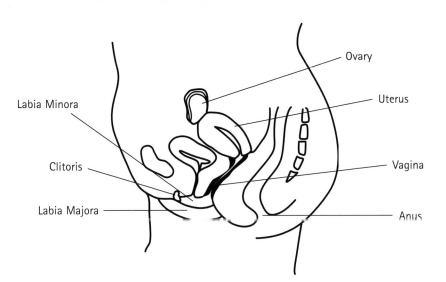

Labia Minora — Ovary — Uterus — Clitoris — Vagina — Labia Majora — Anus

Use a mirror and have a good look at your vagina

SEXPLORATION FOR WOMEN

Start by having a good soak in the tub so you're feeling fresh and relaxed. Now prop yourself up against something firm like a wall, headboard, or pillows. Bend your knees and open your legs to expose your genital area. Position a hand-mirror, propped up against something, so that you can see your genitals while leaving your hands free.

Now take a look at the outer lips. Notice the shape, the texture, and the hair covering. When you open these lips, you will notice the smaller, inner lips. Remember that the appearance of the genitals varies greatly from woman to woman, just as faces do. Your inner lips may be more prominent, perhaps they hang down between the outer lips—this is perfectly normal. The color will also vary. Note your own size and coloring.

Now pull your lips fairly wide apart. This will expose your vagina, urethra, and clitoris. Now gently put your finger inside your vagina (use a little petroleum jelly if you're dry) and see if you can feel the muscle at the entrance, try a couple of squeezes and see if you can feel it. Now see if you can feel a G-spot (remember not all women have one). You will find it about 2 inches inside the vagina on the front wall. Unaroused it may only be the size of a pea, but when you're aroused it can be as big as a penny. You'll notice that, unlike the vaginal walls that are smooth and silky, the G-spot feels rougher, a little like the texture of a walnut. Feel each part in turn. Gently touch, noting texture, temperature and color. When you've finished, take some time to think about anything new that you have learned.

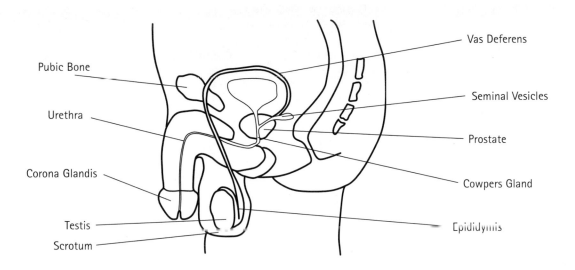

Pubic Bone

Urethra

Corona Glandis

Testis

Scrotum

Vas Deferens

Seminal Vesicles

Prostate

Cowpers Gland

Epididymis

Male genitalia

Boys tend to be fascinated by what's inside their underpants and our vocabulary is full of words to describe what they find. They also quickly learn about cause and effect. From a very young age, they discover that if they touch it or rub it in a certain way, it changes size. Men also learn from an early age that all genitals are different. From the school showers to when they pee, they have ample opportunity to compare themselves with others.

As you can see from the diagram opposite, the unaroused penis is naturally soft and floppy. The average size is around three to four inches, though this varies quite considerably. The glans is the most sensitive part of the penis (corresponding to the female clitoris) and is protected by the foreskin, unless you've been circumcised. When the penis is unaroused, the foreskin completely covers the glans except for the urethral opening where urine is passed. The frenulum is the name for the fold of skin on the underside of the penis between the shaft and the glans. In many men, this is a highly sensitive and pleasurable area. The ridge around the base

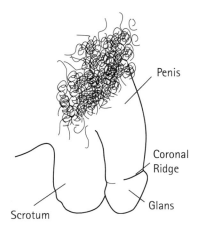

Penis

Coronal Ridge

Glans

Scrotum

of the glans is also extremely sensitive and some men find that gentle pressure on this area can help to delay ejaculation. The scrotum is the sack of skin that contains the two testicles in which sperm are produced.

You may have seen diagrams like this during sex ed. at school. You might remember being told that the testes were sperm-producing factories and that the sperm is then stored in the epididymis until needed. The sperm fluid is produced in the seminal vesicles and the prostate, that is also full of sensitive nerve endings. You can see the vas deferens, the tube that leads to the urethra from which the sperm is released. I'll tell you more about the Cowpers Gland later in the book.

SEXPLORATION FOR MEN

You may think that you already know everything there is to know about your genitals, but many men find it helpful to have a look from a different angle. Start by having a good soak in the tub so you're feeling fresh and relaxed. Now make yourself comfortable and using a hand-mirror, begin to examine your genitals. If you press in above your penis you can feel your pubic bone. Now place your thumb behind and one finger in front of your scrotum, just below the penis and above the testicle. Squeeze gently and you will feel the tube that connects the testes to the urethra, near the base of the bladder (*vas deferens*). Now gently stroke your penis, scrotum, and the area behind your scrotum (*perineum*). Feel each part in turn. Gently touch, noting texture, temperature, and color. When you've finished, take some time to think about anything new that you have learned.

Sexual arousal

Let's take a look at what occurs when you become sexually excited. It's believed that there are four physical stages in sexual arousal: Excitement, plateau, orgasm, and resolution—and our bodies change as we gradually build up through them.

The stages are:

Excitement

This is when your body first begins to respond to sexual thoughts or sexual stimulation. Your heart rate increases as blood is pumped around the body, starting to fill all the small capillaries. As well as feelings of fullness in the genitals, it's also very common to get a blocked nose! Your face and neck may flush and nipples become erect. Breathing becomes heavier as extra oxygen is pumped to your tensing muscles.

Plateau

This is the stage when your body is highly aroused and on the verge of orgasm. Your heart rate and breathing continue to increase as muscles increasingly tense and are ready for release. Most people say that the longer they can stay moving between the excitement and the plateau stages, the stronger their orgasm will feel.

Orgasm

The explosive release of tension. When you orgasm, your pelvic floor muscles will contract between five and 15 times at 0.8-second intervals. This may be accompanied by ejaculation—but not necessarily (more on this later in the book).

Resolution

This is the final stage of the process. Your body begins to relax and return to normal and men enter a refractory period (see page 37). But even now, the woman's body, in particular, goes through some pretty amazing changes (as you will see overleaf).

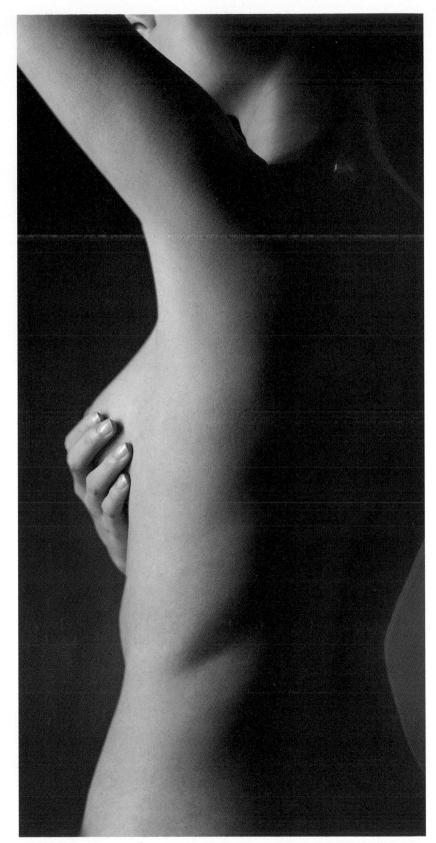

Women are more likely to be multi-orgasmic because, unlike men, they have no refractory period

Stages of female arousal

Excitement

The clitoris is engorged with blood and becomes erect and highly sensitive.

Breasts may increase in size by up to 50%.

The inner and outer lips fill with blood, increase in size, and lift and separate to reveal the vagina.

The upper two-thirds of the vagina begin to lubricate and this slowly slides down the vagina on to the external lips. This lubrication varies in quantity and texture at different times of the month.

The vagina becomes longer and wider, ready to accommodate the penis.

Plateau

The vagina continues to expand, and balloons at the top to form a seminal pool (find out why next).

The uterus lifts into a "false" body cavity to protect it from being buffeted by a thrusting penis.

The clitoris retracts behind the clitoral hood. It is possible that for some women it is too sensitive for direct stimulation.

The lower third of the vagina becomes heavily congested with blood and pelvic floor muscles begin to tighten forming what is known as the "orgasmic platform."

Orgasm

Some women may experience ejaculation. This may be from the G-spot or excess lubrication being expelled by the contractions.

The orgasmic platform pulsates.

PC muscles, uterus, and rectal muscles all contract at 0.8-second intervals.

Resolution

The uterus descends from its "false" position and the cervix dips into the seminal pool to draw semen into the uterus.

The cervix continues to remain open for a further 20–30 minutes.

The clitoris begins to descend to the usual position.

The vagina begins to return to normal size, though the lower third returns more quickly than the upper two-thirds.

Inner and outer lips return to usual size.

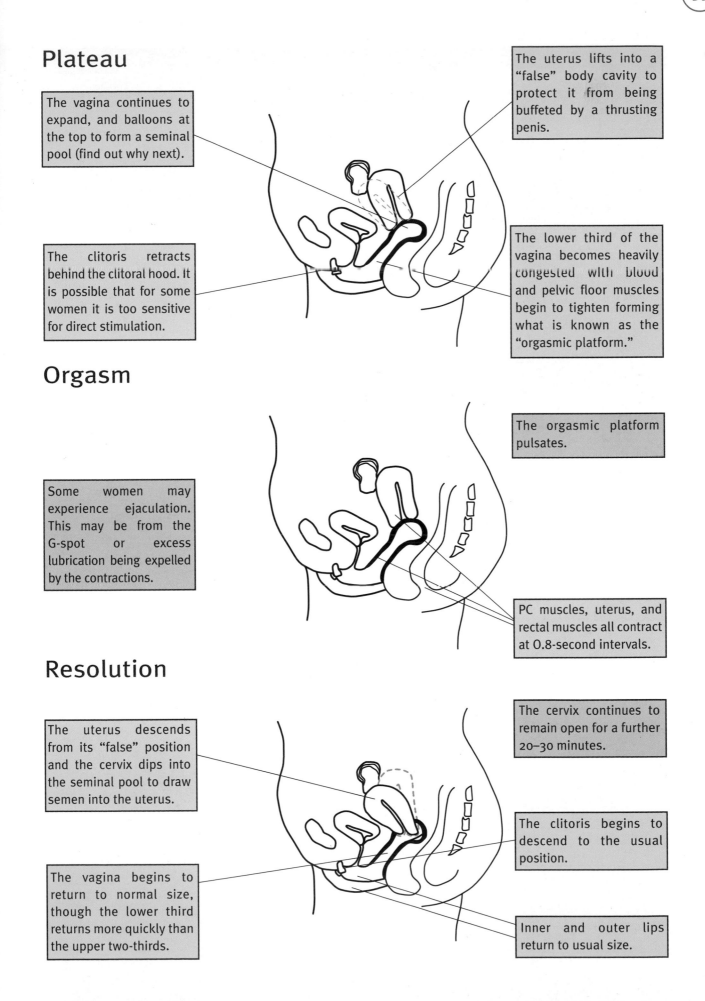

Stages of male arousal

Excitement

Penis engorges with blood and becomes erect. The average male erection is 6 inches long, though this varies greatly.

Some eastern mystics and sports coaches believe that ejaculate is so full of essential nutrients that it should be retained whenever possible. This is also used as an explanation of why men so often fall asleep straight after sex.

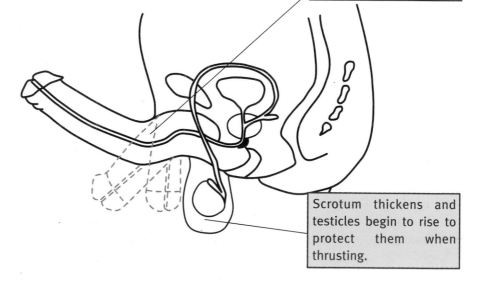

Scrotum thickens and testicles begin to rise to protect them when thrusting.

Plateau

Penis reaches full erection size and the glans increases in diameter and deepens in color.

Cowpers Gland secretes a fluid that both lubricates and cleans the urethra (often known as pre–cum).

Urethra increases in diameter.

Testes become fully elevated and may increase in size by up to 50% (when the testes have fully elevated, ejaculation is imminent).

Orgasm

The prostate, vas deferens, and seminal vesicles contract and collect the ejaculate in the urethral bulb. This is often referred to as the point of inevitability.

The penis and pelvic muscles contract at 0.8-second intervals and force out the ejaculate.

NB: It is possible to orgasm without ejaculating and vice versa, though this is relatively rare.

Resolution

Half of the erection is lost quickly then the rest gradually subsides.

Scrotum returns to normal.

During the resolution phase, men experience the refractory period, when the testes are restocking and preparing to ejaculate again. Until they're ready, the penis will not respond to stimulation. The length of time ranges from a few minutes to hours or even days, depending on health and, more particularly, on age.

Testes lose their swelling and gradually descend.

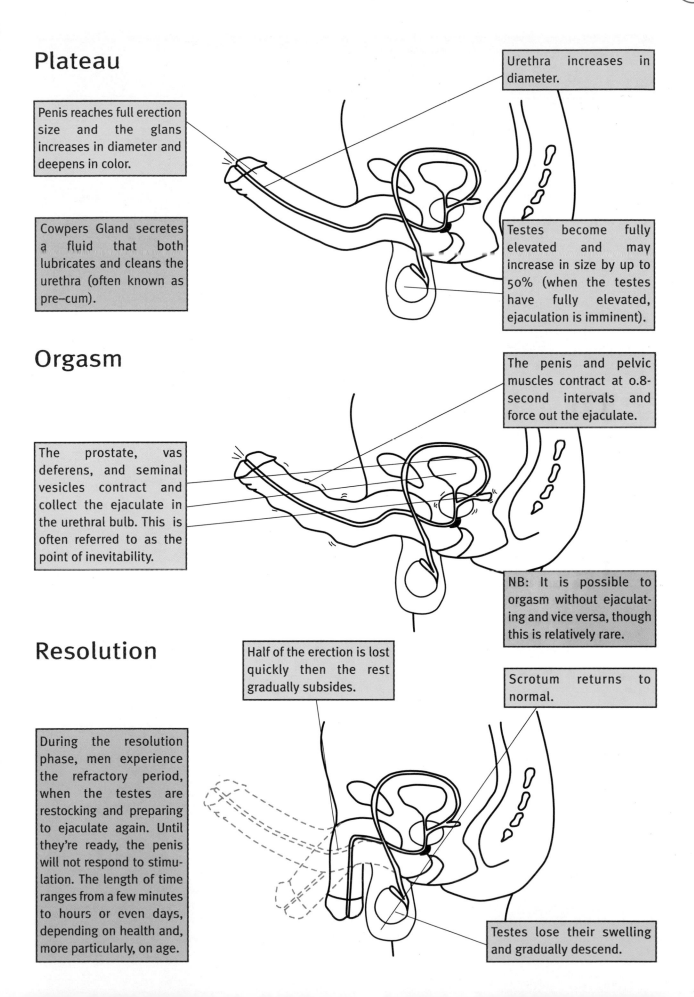

Sexual chemistry

The most influential physical components of our sexuality are our hormones. These microscopic molecules affect our sexual attraction, our sex drives, and sexual behavior. Here, we consider the chemistry of attraction, of desire and the differences in male and female sex drive.

Chemistry of attraction

When eyes meet across a crowded room, and the body is filled with a surge of love or lust, it's not just all in the mind. A whole cocktail of chemicals is released, leaving you feeling dizzy with delight and desperate to get closer.

One of those chemicals is PEA (phenylethylamine). It is released when we see someone we're strongly attracted to. PEA is known as the molecule of love. Italian scientists found large quantities of it in the bloodstreams of lovers and noted that it had a similar impact on behavior to that of people who suffer from obsessive compulsive disorders. The overwhelming desire to be together, to touch, to make love, all seem to be driven by PEA.

The pheromones are another key set of chemicals. They produce a powerful, odorous substance that is still not fully understood. We're aren't even sure where in the body the pheromones are produced but research shows that they have a powerful unconscious affect on other people. Not only do they influence sexual attraction, but they can even affect ovulation and create feelings of wellbeing and intimacy.

The remaining chemical in the attraction cocktail is oxytocin. This is released by breast-feeding mothers and also by lovers when they touch. Oxytocin is responsible for human bonding and the great thing about it is that we can directly influence its production. The more you touch your partner, the more oxytocin you release and the closer you will feel. The closer you feel, the more oxytocin you release, and the more you will want to touch your partner.

PEA can be found in chocolate, which may explain why lovers buy each other chocolate

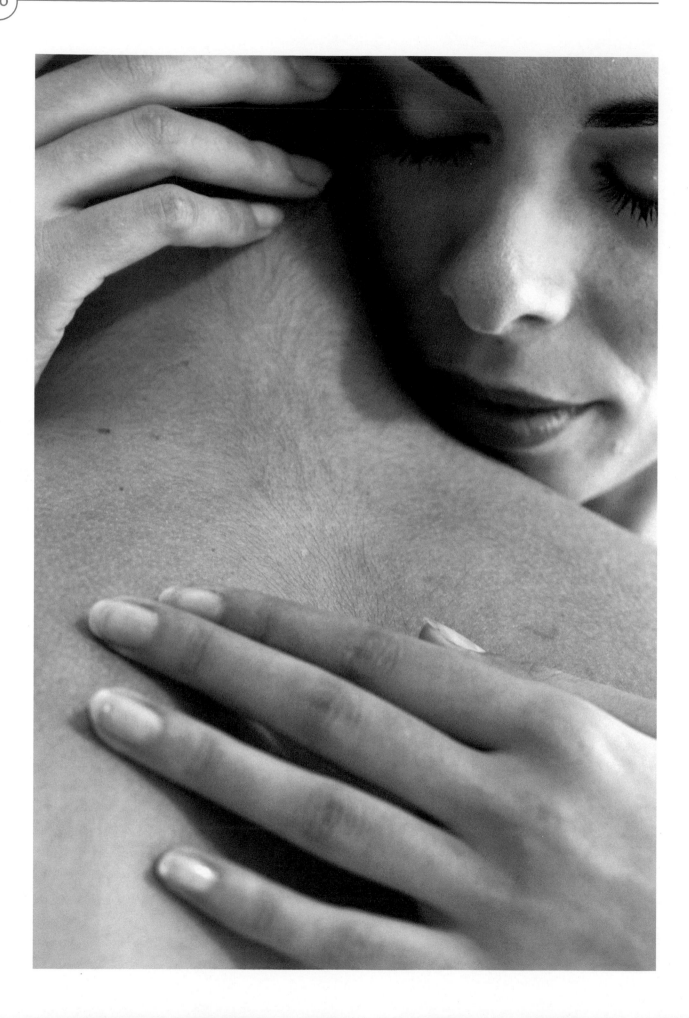

Chemistry of desire

Over and over again, research tells us that men think about sex more often than women. But it's worth noting that, contrary to popular belief, these thoughts are not always welcome turn-ons. Many men describe these intrusive and unwelcome thoughts as downright irritating.

The chemical responsible for this is testosterone and men have 20–40 times more of the stuff than women do. And, more importantly, men's testosterone levels stay pretty much the same throughout their life. For women, testosterone levels are dramatically affected by menstruation and childbearing. For many women there is a marked increase in desire around ovulation when testosterone levels are at their highest.

Other chemicals that influence sexual desire are dopamine and serotonin. Dopamine is responsible for motivating us to seek out pleasure while serotonin decreases anxiety and generates warm, friendly feelings. Having these chemicals in a healthy balance is essential for our general emotional wellbeing as well as for sexual desire. Too little dopamine can make us apathetic and too much can make us pleasure addicts. Too little serotonin can make us anxious and irritable but too much will make us so laid back that we won't care if we never have sex again!

Differences in male and female sex drive

It's not just that men generally want more sex than women, it's also the way that they go about getting it.

The male sex drive, governed by testosterone, tends to be proactive and assertive, even aggressive at times. Testosterone seeks genital pleasure, increases sexual thoughts and fantasies, and responds to novelty. Research supports this by showing that men have more sexual partners, are more likely to pay for sex, have fetishes, and view pornography more often than women. Testosterone also promotes separateness and independence, which might explain why men tend to masturbate more.

A women's sex drive is heavily influenced by estrogen as well as by testosterone. Estrogen is responsible for femininity and seeks intimacy. Not only does it give women their curves but it also gives them their powers of seduction. Unlike the assertive drive of testosterone, estrogen is more receptive. That doesn't mean it's passive, more that it inspires women to be ready, willing, and seductive.

However, because levels of estrogen alter during the menstrual cycle, a woman's sex drive is much more complicated than a man's and can change dramatically over the month. A week of the "seductive sex kitten" might be followed by the more passive "take me, I'm yours." Then you can look forward to a week of "no way José" before ending with a "get here now" or perhaps, "where's my vibrator?" No wonder men are frequently confused!

So, if the sex drives are so different, does that mean men enjoy sex more than women? Absolutely not. Physically speaking, women can enjoy sex more than men since they are capable of multiple orgasms. But great sex isn't just about orgasms, it's also about intimacy and eroticism.

Rather ironically, two of the biggest causes of low sexual desire are depression and anti-depressants, both of which impact dopamine and serotonin levels. If you think either of these could be a problem for you, check with your physician.

It's the mind that has the final say as to whether or not we want sex

Men generally have a stronger and more persistent desire for sex, but once a woman is sexually aroused, her drive for satiation is likely to be every bit as powerful as a man's.

Sexual health

Good sexual health is essential for great sex. When you're confident that there will be no negative consequences, you can relax and fully enjoy the sexual experience. Here is a brief guide to the range of most regularly available contraception and a look at how to avoid sexually transmitted (social) diseases.

Contraception

A increasingly wide choice of contraceptive methods is available. Before you make any decision about which method is right for you, be sure to discuss it with your partner—and also your doctor, if necessary. You can also get advice from a family planning clinic, or the genitourinary clinic of your local hospital. You can find more details in the Helping Agencies section at the back of this book.

Here is a brief guide to the commonest options available.

Barrier methods

The most common are the male condom, the female condom, and the diaphragm. Barrier methods are popular because they are readily available, provide additional protection against sexually transmitted infections, and have no side effects. The most common complaint is that they can be a bit tricky to use, and you have to make sure you always have one with you. It's recommended that each method is used in conjunction with a contraceptive cream or gel.

Intrauterine devices

This is the general name given to contraceptives that are fitted by a health professional into the uterus. The key advantage is that they provide ongoing protection against pregnancy for up to five years, but they can sometimes cause heavier or more painful periods. They're not recommended for all women, so you are advised to have a health check first.

Hormone options

These are perhaps the fastest growing range of options currently available. The contraceptive pill is still a popular choice for many women. It provides good protection against pregnancy, is easy to take, and is effective for as long as the pill is being taken. For women who don't want the responsibility of remembering to take a pill every day, there is the contraceptive injection, implant, or patch, that provide protection over a longer period of time. The disadvantage of the hormone options is that they're not suitable for some women and they may cause troublesome side effects.

Natural methods

There are now a number of quite sophisticated ways of determining when a woman is most fertile. By measuring body temperature, cervical secretions, and/or hormone levels, a couple can agree to abstain from intercourse during the high-risk ovulation period. The system is popular for those who don't like medical intervention but it relies on stringent monitoring, good organization, and a lot of will-power.

Permanent methods

If you're absolutely sure you never want to have children then sterilization is an option. Male sterilization (vasectomy) is a more straightforward procedure than female sterilization and has a quicker recovery rate. Consult your physician for more information.

Sexual health

Sexually transmitted infections (STIs) are on the increase, so it makes sense to make sure you're safe.

Most people would not knowingly pass on an infection, but there are a number of STIs that have few or no symptoms. So a person carrying an STI may have no idea they are putting you at risk. That's why it's essential you take responsibility for your own sexual health. Remember, you don't have to have a lot of sexual partners to get an STI. Unprotected sex with just one infected person is enough.

How to avoid sexually transmitted infections

Regular use of a condom (male or female) when having sex will prevent the transmission of most STIs, including HIV-AIDS. There are more steps you can take that will make sex even safer.

Firstly, make sure you're prepared. Have lots of condoms ready (a huge range is available to add extra interest) and make sure you and your partner have talked about using them before you start and had a few practices at putting one on.

Secondly, be as informed about STIs as you possibly can. You can find a list of common symptoms in Chapter 11. You can also receive routine free checkups at your local health center or GUM (Genito-Urinary Medicine) clinic, usually part of a hospital.

EMERGENCY CONTRACEPTION

Emergency contraception, or the morning after pill as it's sometimes called, is available from your doctor, family planning clinic, and over the counter at most drugstores. It must be taken within three days of having unprotected sex and is more effective the sooner you take it.

Getting in the mood

Each of us has to take responsibility for our own sex drive. Great sex can only happen when we're feeling good about ourselves, fully in touch with our senses, and relaxed and comfortable with our partner. This chapter will help you to create the conditions you need for great sex.

Relaxation

It seems that, in spite of a growing range of labor-saving devices and leisure activities, our lives are becoming busier and busier. For many people, this can lead to stress. When we're stressed it's unlikely that we're going to be interested in sex at all, let alone be able to enjoy great sex. Not only does stress leave us feeling physically drained and exhausted, it also distracts our minds with troublesome thoughts and worries.

Avoiding stress

There are hundreds, if not thousands, of stress management techniques available on the market, but by far the best treatment is to avoid stress in the first place. Stress is an inevitable factor of modern life, however, but you can take sensible steps to stop it accumulating.

Try the following ten tips to keep stress at bay

1. Say No. Protecting your own health and your own relationships is more important than pleasing everyone else, so sometimes, just say no.

2. Be kind to yourself. This means treating yourself as you would your best friend. Remind yourself what a nice person you are and make sure no-one's taking advantage of you—including yourself!

3. Don't be a perfectionist. Rather than striving for perfection and beating up on yourself if everything's not 100%, accept that sometimes it's okay for things to be "good enough."

4. Time management. Plan your time carefully and make sure you schedule in times for rest.

5. Don't procrastinate. Stress is often made worse by putting off until tomorrow what you really know you should do today. Bite the bullet and get it done now. You'll save yourself a load of guilt, worry and, of course, stress.

6. Diet. Remember that you are what you eat. A healthy diet will help you to stay in tiptop physical condition and be able to perform at your best and cope with the occasional stressful event.

7. Exercise. It goes with the diet, I'm afraid. Regular exercise keeps you fit and fit bodies handle stress better.

8. Seek support. When you've had a tough day, make sure there's

someone you can talk to. It doesn't matter if it's a colleague from work, a friend, or a family member, just make sure you've got someone who's willing to help you bear the load

9. Laugh. Laughter really is the best medicine. If something's getting you down, turn it around and see the funny side. Laughter not only has a positive impact on your mental health, but research shows it improves your physical health too.

10. Relax. Easier said that done, I know, but find, by any means necessary, space and time in your life to reflect and relax.

BURNOUT WARNING SIGNS

Burnout is a state of mental, physical, and emotional exhaustion that's brought on by continued stress. Untreated, burnout can lead to depression, so if you're suffering with the following, see your doctor now and get some help.

Irritability—growing impatience and short temper to those around you.

Paranoia—feeling that someone is "out to get you."

Arrogance—a growing sense that only you can do your job and the world couldn't cope without you.

Disorientation—difficulty in concentrating.

Physical complaints—such as headaches, stomach problems, backache, lingering colds.

Feeling unappreciated—growing feelings of bitterness, anger, and resentment toward others.

Exhaustion—lack of energy and tiredness, difficulty keeping up with normal activities.

Detachment—feeling left out or deliberately avoiding spending time with people.

Boredom or Cynicism—questioning the value of friendships, activities, and even life itself.

Changing work style—either becoming bossy and demanding or withdrawing and preferring to work alone and avoid decision-making.

Imagine a peaceful relaxing scene

Learning to relax

Learning how to relax is a skill that can help you in every area of your life—not just your sex life. There are a number of different methods of relaxation, but all of them broadly work in the same way. The aim is to relax muscular tensions, slow down breathing and heart rate, and empty the mind of negative thoughts. What follows is a just a brief outline of the most common relaxation techniques.

Deep breathing

This is a very simple but extremely effective method of relaxation. It's also the core component of most of the more advanced forms. By learning to breathe slowly and deliberately, you can slow down your heart rate and relax tense muscles. The most common method taught is to breathe in through your nose for a count of three and then breathe out through your mouth for a count of six. Make sure you completely fill and empty your lungs each time, and concentrate on the sensation of breathing. Counting as you gently breathe in, and again as you gently breathe out, will help you to fully focus. I know it sounds too simple to be true, but if you only learn one technique, make it this one.

Progressive muscular relaxation

The basic principle is that, when you tense a muscle and then relax it, it will relax to an even greater extent than originally. You can work through your whole body, starting with your toes and gradually working up through your legs, your abdomen, your shoulders, arms, neck, and finally your face muscles. Tense each group of muscles so that they are as tightly contracted as possible. Hold them in a state of extreme tension for a few seconds. Then, relax them to their previous state.

Meditation

Again this is a very simple and effective way of relaxing. Since it's impossible to think of two things at once, by focusing attention on an inanimate object you empty your mind of negative thoughts. You might choose to focus on an object in your home. A common choice is to get something simple like an apple and look at it. But not just look. Really, really look. Notice the color differences, the shape. Now pick it up and think about the texture, the temperature, the way it feels in your hand. If you like you could use a favorite picture or photograph, or a simple candle flame.

An alternative is to focus your attention on listening to a sound. This could be a relaxation tape, or a sound that's around you in nature. Some people focus on a sound that they make, or by reciting a calming line or mantra to themselves. One of the most famous in the world is the Om meditation. Om is a Sanskrit word meaning perfection. Simply repeating the word over and over and over again can bring great waves of peace and relaxation.

Visualization

This is a favorite of mine and a technique that, once mastered, can be developed to enhance sexual fantasies.

To start with, all you need do is close your eyes and imagine a peaceful, relaxing scene. It might be somewhere you've actually been, such as a favorite beach or woodland clearing. Then you recreate the image in your mind by building as much detail as possible. The more senses you use, the more real the image will become. So think not only about what you can see, the colors, the shapes, but also imagine what you can smell and what you can hear. Finally, think about what you can feel, the warmth of the sun, the breeze in your hair. Once you've created somewhere, you can keep the picture in your mind to return to whenever you're feeling stressed.

RELAXATION EXERCISE

Begin by setting aside 10–20 minutes when you know you won't be disturbed. Now...

Sit quietly and comfortably. Close your eyes. Start by focusing on your breathing. Breathe slowly in through your nose for a count of three and gently out through your mouth for a count of six.

Continue for a few moments, becoming aware of how your rib cage expands with the in breath and dilates on the out breath.

Relax the muscles of your body by contracting each set of muscles for a count of four, then relax. Start with your feet and work up the body relaxing your muscles.

Now spend a few more moments focusing on breathing as before, counting the in breath and the out breath.

Now imagine yourself on the most beautiful beach in the world. Look around you, what can you see? Imagine the palm trees or the cliff tops, the sand, the waves.

Now focus on what you can hear. The sound of lapping waves, the seagulls overhead. Smell the saltiness of the sea air. Feel the breeze on your face, the sand beneath your toes, the sun on your skin. Stay here, relaxing for as long as you want to, absorbing the beauty of your surroundings.

In your own time, become aware of your breathing again and, when you're ready, open your eyes and get on with your day.

Intimacy

Good sex means feeling comfortable and confident with your sexual partner. For most people, that will mean that the best sex they have will always be with someone they know well and have a committed relationship with. For others, that intimacy is created more easily with someone who knows little or nothing about them. But for each, intimacy is about feeling able to be open and honest about who you are and how you feel.

Building intimacy

Making time to be together is the best thing you can do to build intimacy in your relationship. There's an old saying: "Love is best spelt T.I.M.E." When you spend time with someone, you're saying how important they are to you. You're saying that other things can wait, your relationship is the priority. It doesn't matter how you spend that time, whether it's going for a walk, doing a household chore, talking, or simply being alongside each other. This strengthens the sense of being a couple.

There's another adage: "Women need to feel close to have sex, and men need to have sex to feel close." Personally I think that's a huge generalization, but there's no doubt that for many people, "feeling close" is essential before they can take off their clothes. You need to work out for yourself how important intimacy is for you in order to have great sex, and how important it is for your partner. If it's important to either of you, then the best investment you can make in your sex life is in spending time together.

TALK AND LISTEN EXERCISE

This is a well-known exercise set by marriage guidance counselors to help build communication skills. Give it a try, and if you find it useful, set aside a regular time to practice it.

Each of you should talk for 30 minutes while the other one gives you their undivided attention. It is essential that after your hour is up that you don't analyze the conversation. In fact, it works best if you agree not to talk about the exercise for at least 48 hours.

Start by tossing a coin to see who is going to get the first half hour. When your time is up, swap roles.

If you're the talker
• You have to take your full 30 minutes, even if you run out of things to say. The silences will give you chance to reflect on what you've said and move deeper.
• Talk about whatever's on your mind—but don't turn it into a moaning session.
• Try to talk only about your feelings and opinions by starting sentences with the word "I."
• If you're the second person to speak, try not to respond to what your partner has just said.

If you're the listener
• Listen attentively and give your partner 100% of your attention.
• Show that you are listening with your body language. For example: Eye contact, nodding, etc.
• You must listen in silence. You can ask for clarification if you don't understand something, but that's all.

Be calm, focused, and keep listening

Better communication

Improving the quality of your communication is undoubtedly the second most important ingredient for building intimacy. To feel known and accepted is one of the most fundamental human needs. Verbal communication is the tool we use to do that. Becoming a good listener and an open, honest talker are essential skills for good communication. The following are some useful tips:

Listen attentively

When you're listening, don't just listen with your ears. Show your partner that you're listening to them by giving him or her 100% of your attention.

Empathise

Show that you really care by putting yourself in your partner's shoes. Feel what they're feeling and let them know it.

Check out

Check that you're really hearing what your partner is saying by checking out important details. So, if necessary, interrupt them and say: "So you're saying that."

When you hear them reply: "Exactly," then you'll both know you've heard right.

Explain yourself

When you're talking, be ready to offer as much information as your partner needs in order to understand your point of view.

Express yourself

As well as giving the facts, make sure that you share your feelings, both good and bad.

Resolving conflict

It's important to accept that differences of opinion are a normal part of human relationships. Each of us is created as a unique individual and therefore conflicting views are inevitable. More often than not, you'll be able to resolve your differences amicably without them affecting your sex life. But if issues linger, one or both of you might find that that as the tension rises, your sex drive goes down.

When differences arise, the first thing you need to do is take responsibility for how you handle it. No one can make their partner better at handling conflict. All you can do is change yourself. Next time you find yourself starting to quarrel, consider the following:

Own your feelings

Your partner cannot make you feel something. Our feelings are under our own control. If you're angry, say "I'm angry because..." not: "You made me angry..."

Assume the best

Rather than assuming the worst possible motives, thoughts, and feelings of your partner, assume the best. You may later get evidence to the contrary, but until that time, always give your partner the benefit of the doubt.

Check your conscience

Is this argument happening because there's something you're avoiding doing, such as apologizing, compromising, or forgiving? Make sure you're not fighting to protect your pride.

Check your environment

Don't underestimate the power of external circumstances. Are you feeling stressed, tired, hormonal, or angry at something outside your relationship?

Be adult

Do you tend to slip into behaving like a child, sulking, whining, blaming, or obstinacy. Or do you become like a critical parent, condescending, criticizing, or punishing. An adult should be calm, focused, and good at listening and negotiating.

> **The best investment you can make for your sex life is time together**

INTIMACY REQUESTS

This is another exercise used by marriage guidance counselors.

You and your partner take it in turns, on alternate days of the week, to be the Requester. The Requester is going to think of an intimate request to make from their partner during that day. The request should be an action that can be realistically achieved during the day. For example, it could be "go for a walk with me," "phone me at lunchtime," "watch something on TV with me," "buy me flowers," and so on. NB: It can not be sexual (that comes later...)

The person being asked is allowed to say "no" and occasionally there may be a good reason for that, in which case a different request can be made. If there isn't a good reason, then you wait until it's your turn to be the Requester again. Of course, it rarely happens that a partner says no, because they know that if they do, that there's little chance of them having their request accepted tomorrow!

The reason this exercise is so successful is that it encourages couples to think about what they need from their partners and ask for it. Over time, you'll find it becomes a natural part of your daily lives and you can drop the formality of taking turns.

Sensuality

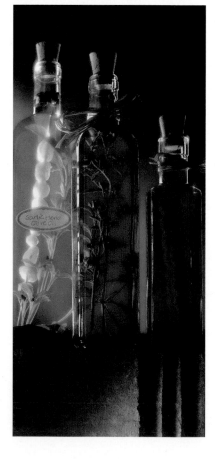

Great sex is not just about physical intimacy. It means using all of your senses, getting in touch with the pleasures that can be ours when we use our eyes, ears, nose, mouths, and of course, the biggest sensory organ we have, our skin. The next chapter contains tips on exploring your sensuality together, but for now, I want you to focus on feeling sensual on your own by concentrating on how your body feels.

When you take time to focus on your senses, your sensory awareness increases. The lightest touch that might have left you cold previously can send shivers of delight down your spine.

Open your eyes

All lovers know that candlelight is great if you've got a less-than-perfect body—and let's face it, most of us have! And most people know that it creates a relaxing and calming mood as well. But did you know that color can have an equally powerful effect? Red is traditionally the color of lovers because it increases heart and respiration rate and is believed to excite the sexual organs. But how about experimenting with these:

Black stimulates self-confidence, power, and strength.

Blue lowers blood pressure, decreases respiration, and generally has a calming effect.

Green aids mental and physical relaxation. It is also particularly beneficial for people suffering from anxiety, nervousness, or depression.

Violet suppresses appetite, provides a peaceful environment, and helps reduce migraines.

Pink is also an appetite-suppressant, relaxes muscles, and relieves tension.

Yellow and orange both energize, stimulate appetite, and relieve depression. Additionally, yellow is believed to improve memory.

A SENSUAL TREAT

Start by running yourself a deep, warm bath. Now add your favorite bath foam or oil, step in, and relax.

Now take some time to really focus on the warmth of the water. Does the temperature feel different on different parts of your body? How does the water feel as it moves over your skin? Notice the varying textures of your skin and the areas that are most sensitive to touch. How do the bubbles or oil feel against your skin? Does it tickle in some places? Is it soft and warming?

When you've had enough, get out of the tub and begin to dry yourself with a warm towel. But rather than just using the towel to get dry, focus on how the towel feels on different parts of your body. Do you prefer being dried gently? Or firmly? Or vigorously?

When you're dry, take some time to smooth on your favorite body lotion. And as you're doing it, explore your body from head to toe. Think about what kind of touch different parts of your body enjoy. Experiment with different pressures and strokes, noticing which direction your body prefers. Spend some time touching your chest. Move your hands down your body to focus on your stomach, hips, and butt, finishing with your inner thighs.

Open your ears

What kind of music gets you in the mood? And what sort of mood does it get you into? Flick through your music collection and see if you can discover the beats that energize you, as well as the melodies that soothe and relax. Which are the tunes that make you want to socialize and chat and the sounds that make you want to make love? Music will affect you differently on different days, but see if you can find your personal top five, guaranteed to put you in the mood for love.

Sensual smells

If you don't have an aromatherapy burner then buy one today. A vast range of essential oils is available that can enhance or even change moods. Choose lavender for relaxation, ylang ylang for sensuality, bergamot to be uplifted

and enlivened, camomile to relieve stress, and sandalwood to boost your sexual energy.

A matter of taste

The link between food and sex has existed for centuries. Our tongues are packed with nerve-endings and as well as tasting food, our tongue also enjoys the sensual texture and feel of food in our mouths. Next time you've got nothing to do for an evening, visit your local deli and let your tongue go wild.

And finally—touch

Studies have shown that without touch, many animals, including humans, will die in childhood. Being caressed lowers blood pressure and releases natural opiates in the brain that are associated with a relaxed frame of mind. Human touch has the power to comfort and support, to protect, to encourage, to relax and of course, to arouse. Touching is crucial if you want to be a good lover and so is learning how to fully enjoy being touched. Next time you take a bath, spend some time really focusing on the physical sensations of your skin. Also think about how different textures feel on your body. The smooth, cool texture of silk, the warm comfort of a fleecy blanket, the delicate tickling of feathers.

Isn't it time you came to your senses?

Don't save pretty undies for special occasions. Wear them every day and enjoy the sensual feel against your skin.

Getting in touch with your sensuality will not only increase pleasure while you are being touched, it will also inspire you to touch your partner in places and ways you'd never thought of before. So, isn't it time you came to your senses?

A SENSUAL TREAT
WEARING LINGERIE

Lingerie should not just be something women wear to make themselves attractive to men. Whether you're male or female, the sensation of silk or satin on your skin can be a sensual delight and an all-day reminder of the joys of a gentle, intimate caress.

Exciting yourself

Your partner is not responsible for your sex drive. Hopefully, there will be times when you are driven wild with passion but there'll also be times when sex is the furthest thing from your mind. But ultimately, you are responsible for making yourself sexually aware, sexually alert, and sexually responsive.

Assuming you're feeling reasonably relaxed, both physically and mentally, and your mind isn't preoccupied, it's time to get your brain thinking about sex.

Sexual memories

The first tool in your kitbag is your own sexual history. You don't need any props or too much imagination for this, just your memory. The simplest way to excite yourself is to create a space in which those memories can come flooding back.

Set some time aside over the coming few days to rake through your memory banks and select your top three sexual encounters. They may be times with a current partner, or they may have been with someone else. It might be linked to a particular occasion such as birthday, anniversary, or party you were at or perhaps while you were on vacation. You might remember a long, lingering evening when you made love into the early hours or an impromptu grope in the office stationery closet.

Whatever the occasion was, allow your memory to recreate the scene in as much detail as possible. If you find it useful, you could write it down—your very own true erotic story. Now really take some time to remember the physical sensations. Remember the sensation of arousal, your breathing, your yearning. Remember how it felt when you were touched and as you touched your lover. Remember the sensations as your body built to an erotic crescendo. And finally, remember the feelings of release and relief as the passion ebbed from your bodies.

Now put those memories in a jar and place them on a shelf in

your mind where you can find them anytime you need them. Next time you're in the tub, or you're waiting for your lover to come to bed, take the jar from the shelf, open it, and enjoy all over again.

You alone are responsible for your sex drive

10 WAYS TO GET IN THE MOOD

1. Relax in a long, sensual bath.
2. Relive an erotic memory.
3. Listen to some mood music.
4. Wear sexy, sensual lingerie.
5. Read an erotic story.
6. Watch a stimulating video.
7. Touch and caress a nude sculpture.
8. Slip into your favorite fantasy.
9. Treat yourself to a massage.
10. Put some ylang ylang in the burner, get something delicious to savor from the refrigerator, and browse through some pictures of beautiful bodies.

Ultimately, you are responsible for making yourself sexually aware, sexually alert, and sexually responsive

Erotica

Many people find using erotic material—literature and visual images—really helpful for getting themselves in the mood. The brain is stimulated by the information that is put into it. If you spend all your free time reading about fishing and surround yourself with pictures of trout, then fishing is likely to occupy a lot of your gray matter. So if you spend time reading about sex and looking at sensual, sexual images, then you're going to think about sex a lot more often.

It's essential that you find the kind of erotic material that suits your personal taste. Lots of people immediately think of overt centerfolds of busty blonds, but the choice is so much greater than that. There are many magazines around that are more or less sexually explicit, and offer sexual information, images, and stories.

Think also about your bedtime reading, think about exchanging that historical biography for a book containing some sexual intrigue or romance. You can also consider the things you see around your house. How about investing in a nude (or rude) sculpture, photograph, or painting. And there's now a huge choice of sexy and raunchy knicknacks that you can use everyday of the week to keep sex in the forefront of your mind.

Erotica is discussed in greater detail on page 120.

Fantasy

Sexual fantasy is a provocative subject in more ways than one. Some people believe fantasies are a sign of mature, uninhibited sexuality, while others believe they are the exclusive preserve of the lonely and frustrated. How you feel about sexual fantasy will be influenced by your understanding of what a sexual fantasy is. Some people assume a sexual fantasy is always about some sort of suppressed, kinky activity that a person is desperate to act out. That isn't so. Many fantasies are sexually explicit, but a lot are also about romance and intimacy as well. And most fantasies are about an existing partner. ·

An active fantasy life can provide an arena in which to act out things that we might not have the opportunity to do in real life. These opportunities might not arise because of our, or our partner's, inhibitions. Or we might not be able to act them out because either our partner or ourselves aren't physically capable of them. Many fantasies, such as making love on a Caribbean beach or on the deck of our own private yacht won't happen because we simply don't have the dough. Some fantasies are things we enjoy imagining but would never ever want to do in real life, such as making love in a public place or having sex with a stranger. There is a huge range of personal taste in sexual fantasy, but in fantasy, it is a case of no holds barred—no need to fear rejection or retribution.

An active imagination can mean that you're ready for sex before anything physical has even started. So now that your brain's in top gear, it's time to get with the action.

Fantasy is discussed in more detail on page 136.

In fantasy there are no holds barred—no need to fear rejection or retribution

---

LEARNING TO FANTASIZE

First of all you need to make sure you're fully relaxed and comfortable. Either sit or lie down and start by using some of the relaxation techniques discussed in the previous chapter.

Once you are feeling physically relaxed, begin to build a picture in your mind's eye of your perfect erotic encounter. As you build your picture, put as much detail into it as possible. Really think about what you can see. Who's there? Just you and a lover, or are others present? What does your lover look like? Their face? Their body? And what about you, what are you wearing? How does your lover look at you? Now think about what you can smell? Is there a fragrance of aftershave or perfume? How does your lover's body smell? Now think about the sounds, how does your lover speak? What do they say? And finally, imagine what you can feel. How does your lover's body feel when you touch it? How does it feel to be kissed? How does it feel when they caress you?

Build as much detail as you can and allow yourself to fully experience every sight, sound, smell, and touch. And when you're ready, come back to the present.

The more regularly you repeat the same fantasy experience, the more detailed and therefore the more powerful it will become. Practice will help it become more perfect!

Making it happen

How we communicate with our partners—both verbally and non-verbally—is the key to making great sex an intrinsic part of our relationships rather than a longed-for fantasy. Here are a few tips on romance and seduction, advice on talking frankly about sex with your partner, and instructions on sensual massage techniques and discovering erogenous zones.

Time for romance

Romance is essential for keeping couples in touch with each other as loving, tender, sensual human beings. So when does romance become seduction? Although the actions may be similar, in seduction the motivation is clear, you're saying: "I want to make love to you."

Romance

All relationships need trust and respect to keep them going but, assuming you have these, romance is the key to a relationship, rather than sliding into routine. Romance stops us from taking each other for granted and reminds you that you have something special.

Now, contrary to what you might think, romance isn't just about buying flowers or chocolates, or something you have to remember once a year on Valentine's Day. Romance encompasses any thoughtful, kind, or fun thing that you do for each other or do together. For example, a romantic gesture can be to help your partner to clean up the yard, remember to buy a favorite food at the supermarket, text you in the middle of the day to say "I'm thinking of you," or snuggle up to you while sharing a tub of ice cream. Romance is any activity that says "You're important to me."

Another point of confusion is whether or not romance should lead to sex. The answer is definitely no. Whether you're enjoying an expensive candlelit dinner at an exclusive restaurant or a simple supper for two in your kitchen, sex should not be the goal. If the only times you indulge in sex is after paying a compliment or completing a household chore, then chances are your sex life together—and possibly your relationship—is not going to last.

Keeping in touch

A simple way of keeping your relationship romantic is to remember to touch each other regularly. That doesn't mean you have to have long, lingering embraces every few minutes (though obviously that's fine if you want to!), but it does mean

taking and making opportunities to touch.

Many couples don't even share the same sofa in the evening when they're watching television. If you're one of them, then tonight's the night to change that routine forever. And if you don't already do so, make sure when you leave the house or come home, you find each other and kiss. This should be the bare minimum amount for every couple on a daily basis.

In addition, consider adding these to your regular repertoire:

A pat on the butt when passing.

A kiss on the back of the neck while your partner's working.

A touch on the arm when you ask a question.

A caress of the thigh while driving.

A hug for no reason at all.

A kiss for no reason at all.

Romance is any activity that says, "You are important to me"

Romance often comes naturally to couples when they first get together. New couples are desperate to touch and since their every waking moment is spent thinking about their partner, thoughtful gestures come automatically.

Kissing

A kiss on the lips is probably going to be the first intimate thing you do with your partner. Kisses on the cheek are a commonplace greeting between friends and family, but a kiss on the lips is something that's generally reserved for lovers.

After the genitals, the lips are the most sensitive part of the body. They're full of nerve-endings and can give and receive hours of pleasure. When a young couple first make out, they'll often spend all night petting. It's a pleasurable thing to do and, at that stage at least, not something that automatically leads to sex. When couples have been together for a while, kissing often becomes just a method of greeting, and the passion and intensity of earlier smooches become a dim and distant memory. But it's never too late to reintroduce the power of the kiss.

Your lips can give and receive hours of pleasure

Kissing with confidence

Some couples seem to fit together well, and kissing immediately feels perfect between them. Others have to work at it, and it's one of those activities that's often hard to encapsulate easily in words, so becoming a better kisser is often a case of trial and error. The key to perfect kissing is to start gently and explore. If your partner reciprocates, then continue, if they draw back, then do something else. Here are some popular techniques:

French kissing

Start by gently exploring your partner's lips with your tongue and as they open up, gradually increase the depth and urgency of your exploration.

Nibble kisses

You have to be very, very gentle with this one, unless you're both into S&M. Gently caress your partner's lips and tongue with little bites.

Chicken kisses

This is when you gently peck your lover over and over again. As well as being sensual, it can also be ticklish and stimulating.

Suction kisses

Suck on your partner's lips or tongue, or even teasingly draw their breath through your mouth.

Teasing kisses

Gently and teasingly kiss your partner on the cheeks, the chin, the eyelids, the nose—in fact anywhere but the mouth. It'll only be a matter of time before they pull you to their lips.

Remember kissing isn't just for lips. Being kissed all over can be a wonderfully intimate and playful way of moving from romance to seduction.

To ensure you're kissable, keep your lips soft and smooth; always ensure your teeth are clean and your breath is fresh

10 INSTANT ROMANTIC GESTURES

1. Leave a loving note in a briefcase, under the windshield, on the computer screen.
2. Send a tender email or text.
3. Hold hands.
4. Give flowers.
5. Sprinkle rose petals on the bed.
6. Hug and talk about your day.
7. Shower together.
8. Draw a kiss on a mirror for your lover to find.
9. Give your partner a surprise kiss and cuddle.
10. Share a hot chocolate and look at the night sky.

Seduction

So when does romance become seduction? In reality, the action might be exactly the same, but in seduction the motivation is clear. Whatever you're doing, you're saying, "I want your body" and, "I want to make love to you." On some occasions, simply saying that you're in the mood for sex will be enough. On other occasions, you might decide that you want to indulge in a little teasing or scene-setting first.

Some of this may be similar to what you do in a romantic mood—lighting candles, playing soothing music, or sharing a delightful meal for instance. But this time your desire is overt. Obviously you can't guarantee that you'll end up making love together, but you're both happy to play the seduction game and see where it leads.

Seduction doesn't have to happen a few hours before a sexual encounter. It can occur throughout the day. With advances in technology, there are now so many ways you can say, "You wait till I get you home tonight!"

Here are just a few suggestions couples can enjoy whenever and where ever they are.

• Send each other raunchy texts throughout the day.

• Whisper the things you're longing to do to their body. This is especially provocative if you're in public and may be overheard.

• Email your plan for tonight's passionate encounter, ensuring, of course, that your mail is secure.

• Discreetly caress a breast, butt, or inner thigh. Again, this is particularly exciting if you're in public and risk being seen.

Start your seduction early

• Drag your partner into the stationery store, the bathroom, or anywhere private for a furtive fumble.

• Wink. It's a classic that's still loaded with sexual innuendo.

• Dance suggestively.

• Pay a sexual compliment, though be discreet if you're in public, for example: "Your breasts look fantastic in that blouse."

• Slip your hand in your partner's pants pocket. It's surprising what you might find.

• Play footsie underneath a table or desk in a public place while in company.

There's no right or wrong way to be sensual. But letting your partner know that you love them and want them sexually will keep the light of passion burning, ready to burst into flame at the slightest touch.

Letting your partner know you want them sexually will keep passion alight

10 ROMANTIC IDEAS FOR AN EVENING IN

1. Snuggle up under the comforter and share a tub of ice cream.
2. Take a bubble bath together and share a bottle of champagne.
3. Give a back or foot rub.
4. Have a picnic in the garden or in front of the fire.
5. Give a massage.
6. Enjoy a candlelit dinner for two.
7. Play some smoochy music and dance the night away together.
8. Watch a romantic movie together.
9. Have a pillow fight.
10. Play a game together.

Sex talk

When it gets down to the nitty-gritty of how to enhance your sex life, body language just isn't enough. Great lovers are people who feel comfortable talking openly and honestly about sex. They're not afraid to ask for what they want or make suggestions for new things they'd like to try. And they welcome any and every opportunity to talk about what they can do to improve their partner's sexual pleasure.

For many people, talking openly about their sexual needs is awkward—or even embarrassing, but like all skills, it's something that becomes easier with practice. It takes courage and commitment to talk openly about your sex life, but however difficult it might seem, it's well worth the effort.

We all need to feel safe before we try something new. And if that something is sexual, we have to feel it's okay to change our minds or say "no." Some people are so scared of disappointing their partner by not sharing their enthusiasm for a sexual activity that they avoid ever trying new things. This is a shame for both partners. Whenever you start a conversation about sex, make sure you reassure your partner that if either of you feels uncomfortable in any way at all, at any time at all, it will be alright to stop without any hard feelings.

Whether you want to talk about stimulation techniques or you want to suggest something new, tact and timing is the key. Be sure that both of you are in a relaxed and settled frame of mind and that your reasons for wanting to raise the subject are purely about improving your sex life, not a subtle way of complaining about aspects of it. Think through what you would like to say and make sure you are open to having a discussion and are willing to offer your partner something, as well as asking for things for yourself.

Timing

The best time to talk about trying new things is not a few seconds before you want to do it. If some exciting and innovative idea enters your mind in the middle of a lovemaking session, it's generally safer to leave it there. Many a night of passion has been wrecked by a carelessly timed

whisper of, "Do you mind if I try this?" Unless you're 100% sure your partner is going to be as enthusiastic as you are about a new toy, new position, or new sexual act, discuss it fully and frankly first.

For some people, the best time to talk about sex is when they're fully dressed and away from the bedroom. When there's absolutely no opportunity for sex, it often feels less threatening. However, it may also feel a little out of place, so you need to think about timing carefully. For example, the middle of a crowded restaurant or at your parents' house might not feel appropriate. Some couples have found the best time is when they're both relaxing together. This might be a Sunday morning late lie-in or relaxing in the evening on the sofa. Wherever you choose to talk, you need to make sure that you have a reasonable amount of time and that you won't be disturbed.

Talking about your sex life takes courage. For many people it doesn't come easily, but the results pay dividends

Tact and timing are the key to successful sex talk

Tact

There are a number of ways of introducing a new idea, but you need to be sure that whatever method you choose, you're not making it sound as if you're unhappy about your sex life together. Rather than saying, "I'd like to make our sex life exciting," say, "I'd like to make our sex life even more exciting." This is particularly important if you want to encourage your partner to stimulate you in a new or different way. Announcing, "I want you to do such-and-such," might be interpreted as, "I don't like what you're doing," or even, "What you're doing isn't good enough." Even if that is the case, your partner is going to be more open to change if the suggestion sounds reasonable. For example, say "I would like us to learn some more ways of pleasing each other."

You may be wondering how to respond if your partner says, "What's wrong with things as they are?" or even, "I'm happy with the way things are." In this situation, remember to be encouraging. The response should be, "Yes, things are good now, but I'd like to make them even better," or "I agree, things are good now but I want to make sure we don't get into a rut." You might add that the reason you're raising the subject isn't that you're unhappy, but that you've recently read an article about it or perhaps read about it in a new book you've bought.

Give and take

Many couples find it helpful to talk about sex in a more structured way, both of you having thought about what you want from your sex life. Because it's a fair exchange of ideas and feelings, both of you can feel more comfortable asking for what you would like. And both of you get the opportunity to say no to the

suggestion the other is making.

One way of doing this is to each take some time alone to write a list of, say, three activities you would like to do either more of, or try for a first time, in your sex life. When each of you has compiled your list, agree a time when you will share what you've written down. Then you need to agree if you will try everything at once or take turns on alternate lovemaking sessions.

Some couples enjoy writing these lists together of all the things they enjoy doing and would like to try together. Then they put all the things in a hat and pick something out each time they make love.

It's important that you find a way of communicating that suits your relationship. And remember, it's essential that both of you feel comfortable and confident enough to say "no" to anything that's not okay at any stage of the proceedings.

Spend time alone to write a list of activities that excite you

OK – NOT OK

Try this simple technique for exploring new things to do with your partner. Get a piece of paper and draw the following.

NOT OK

MIGHT BE OK

OK

Now, with your partner, brainstorm all the sexual practices you can think of. Then mark down each thing in one of the boxes. Anything that's Not OK for either of you is a nono. Those in the Might Be OK box are open for experimentation and those that are OK—if you're not doing them already, try them tonight!

Sensual massage

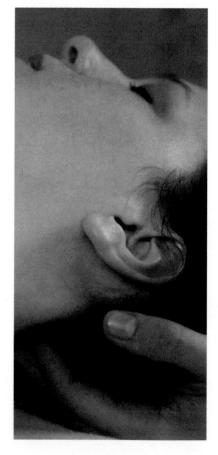

Giving and receiving a sensual massage is a sensitive and sensual way of becoming closer to your partner. Being caressed and stroked will help to put you in a more relaxed frame of mind and may well stimulate you at the same time. Here are a number of tips on preparation and massage strokes.

Preparation

• Set aside at least an hour when you won't be disturbed. Lock the door and unplug the phone.

• Get the room ready by making sure it's warm enough (80°F is considered the optimum). Check that the lighting is suitable. Candlelight is great, but if that's not possible, side-lighting will suffice. You could put a suitable oil in the aromatherapy burner.

• Unless you'd prefer to have the room quiet, choose some relaxing background music.

• Take a bath or shower, or whatever you need to feel relaxed and confident about your body.

• If you're the recipient, do anything you need to be fully relaxed, for example, removing eyeglasses or contact lenses.

• If you are the masseur, make sure your hands are warm and your nails are trimmed.

General tips

• Take your time, relax, and enjoy this intimate time together.

• Use whatever kind of touch and pressure that feels best to your partner. Ask for feedback on what you're doing and adjust your stroke or pressure accordingly.

• Use a massage oil or lotion. Warm it between your hands before applying, and spread it evenly over the body.

• Try to keep all your movements steady and rhythmical. Touch that is predictable is more relaxing than random strokes.

• Keep your hands in constant contact with your partner's skin so when you move to different areas of the body, you do so in a smooth, continuous movement.

If you don't have time for a full body massage, just give your partner a relaxing back rub or foot massage

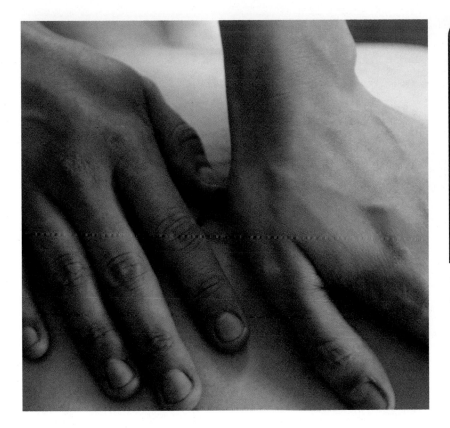

the hands, one following the other, upward along the muscle.

Pulling

Best used on the sides of the torso and on the thighs, with alternate hands simply pulling along the length of the muscle.

Friction

Be gentle in the application of this technique, which is ideal for working on deeper muscles. Use thumbs and fingertips to push into the small muscle groups, making circular movements.

Percussion

As the name implies, this means stimulating the body with rapid bouncing movements. You might use the sides of your hands, known as chopping, or use your hands with the palms downward and cupped, known as cupping. It improves skin tone and circulation but it is important not to use these strokes on the spine as they may be damaging.

Massage strokes

A wide range of different strokes is used in massage. If you wish to become better at massage, invest in a good book or video that is dedicated to the subject. Meanwhile, start by trying some of these techniques:

Gliding

The most basic and common stroke used. Keeping the fingers together and hands outstretched. Simply glide the hands forward along the length of the body or limb. Keep the flat of your hand in contact with the skin. This kind of stroke is best for large areas of the body such as the back, chest, stomach, and thighs.

Circular

Similar to the gliding stroke above, but rather than moving up and down the body, use a circular motion instead.

Fanning

Particularly effective on the back. Involves starting at the base of the spine with hands quite close together and, using the gliding hand motion, move both hands together and allow them to fan out over the sides of the back.

Kneading

Generally a firmer stroke that can help to relieve tired, tense muscles. Gently grasp the area with both hands—say, shoulders, calf, and thigh—and knead with your fingers, tensing and relaxing them.

Draining

Good for the relief of tense muscles. Using either the heel of your hand, or thumbs on smaller muscles, gently, but firmly move

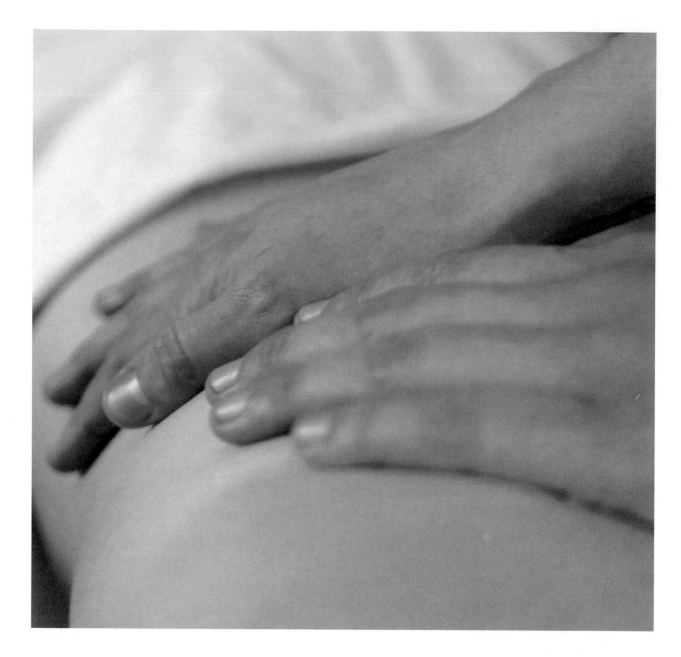

Ask what feels good and what feels best

Erogenous Zones

The most frequently mentioned erogenous zones are the genitals, buttocks, and breasts. But there are many more, but for some people these parts of their body remain a mystery to themselves and their partners.

There are variations in the degree to which touch is erogenous. One day, an unintended caress on the neck can send shivers down your spine, but on another day, it leaves you cold. This is particularly true of women, whose skin sensitivity and receptivity change with the menstrual cycle.

How to find your top five non-genital erogenous zones

Discovering erogenous zones that you didn't know you had is great fun. One of the best ways to find out what and where they are is through sensual touching. But make sure you keep your focus on finding out what turns your partner on rather than what feels relaxing.

Start by looking back at how to prepare for massage and get yourselves set up to spend an evening discovering new and exciting things about yourself and your partner. Take turns to

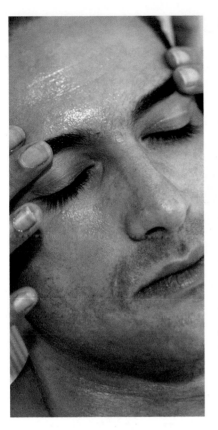

explore each other's bodies, asking for feedback throughout. Try different strokes on different parts of the body—soft, firm, tickles, fingertips, flats of the palms. Experiment, explore, and ask what feels good and what feels best. Try using scaling questions as well. For example, "On a scale of one through 10, how horny does this make you feel?"

When you've worked your way along your partner's back, ask them to roll over and start on their front. Still working from head to toe, experiment, explore and ask for feedback.

The areas you should take time to explore include the inner elbows, backs of knees, the tender skin behind the ears, skin between toes and fingers, feet, back of the neck, and armpits. You'll notice that some of those places will only be arousing if touched in a certain way. A tickle on the neck may send your partner into rapture, but a tickle on the foot could result in a kick in the face.

RUDE FOOD

For something completely different, try and recreate the infamous refrigerator scene from the erotic thriller "9½ Weeks." Start by taking a trip around the supermarket, collecting as wide a range of foods as possible. Choose a selection of textures as well as tastes, sweet, savory, creamy, chalky, sticky. Now take it in turns to blindfold each other and tantalizingly caress your chosen food across your lovers lips. Can they tell what it is from the odor and texture? Then teasingly let your lover lick and savor the flavor. Do they know what it is now, or do they need to take a bite? Remember to have fun, and be kind. No chili peppers allowed!

Giving pleasure

Now we've explored the roles of sexual confidence, sensuality, and intimacy we're ready to look at one of the most significant ingredients—pleasure. This chapter talks about masturbation and gives some hands-on guidance on how to tease and please your partner.

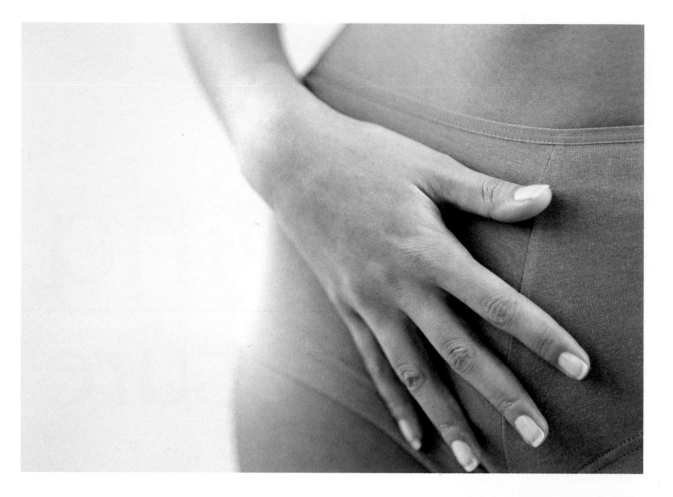

Pleasuring yourself

Many people find masturbation a useful way of exploring their bodies. In complete privacy and with no distractions, you can experiment with different types of touch, different textures on your body, different positions, and include fantasies or erotica if you wish.

Until the dawn of the sexually permissive era in the 1960s, the prevailing ethos of sex books and guides was that masturbation was wrong. Gradually, it became accepted that most adolescent boys masturbated, and this was increasingly considered a phase of sexual development but one to be grown out of in maturity. Slowly, more and more statistics revealed that masturbation was also commonplace amongst men in committed relationships, and in 1972, the American Medical Association finally declared masturbation "a normal activity."

It still took a long time before consideration was given to female masturbation. These days, statistics indicate that either more women are masturbating or that attitudes are changing at last and females are more comfortable admitting to it. Probably it's a combination of both. Finally, it is now generally accepted that masturbation is a healthy and natural pastime for both men and women.

The pendulum now seems to have swung too hard the other way, and certain modern sex guides advise that masturbation is essential for a healthy and liberated sex life. Personally I think that's nonsense. I have met many healthy and liberated men and women who just don't find it satisfying touching themselves. They've tried, but they just can't get· excited enough. If this describes you, you should know that you're perfectly normal and healthy, and can still enjoy great sex with your partner.

For some people, learning from masturbation allows them to create a varied masturbation repertoire. Like sex with a partner, you can choose a quickie or savor a longer, more sensual arousal.

Some lovers enjoy sharing what they've learned about themselves through masturbation by talking to their partners and asking them to try different things next time they make love. Others say nothing until they're in bed and then use their knowledge to guide their partner into new, uncharted territory.

LONG LIVE VARIETY!

If you're without a partner for a long period of time and always masturbate in exactly the same way, then you may inadvertently be creating a problem for yourself in the future. Our genitals can become creatures of habit, and if the only stimulation they receive for months on end is a firm two-handed grip or a vibrator, they may forget how to respond to any other form of stimulation. So make sure you enjoy a variety of touch so when you finally meet the lover of your dreams, you won't have to spend months retraining yourself.

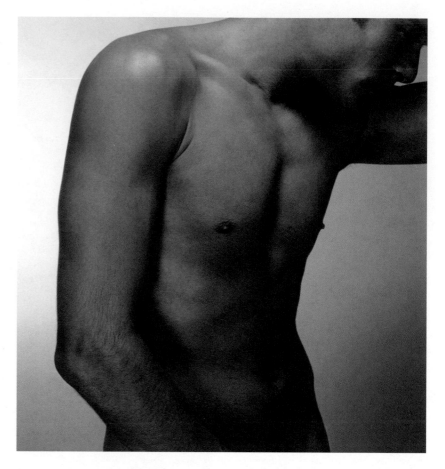

Boys find touching their genitals entirely natural

Men and masturbation

Most surveys conclude that men masturbate more than women. It is true that they have a stronger sexual desire and tend to start at a younger age. Little boys soon discover that when they touch their penis in a certain way it feels good and goes hard, sometimes to the embarrassment of a parent. Boys are also used to touching their penises when they visit the bathroom. So the touching of genitals is seen as a natural and normal thing to do.

It might be several years before a boy first ejaculates and unless he's got some idea that it's going to happen, it can come as quite a shock. But generally, he will have learned from friends or family that this is something that boys do. It's also relatively common for young men to masturbate in groups, either just for the sheer fun of it, or to compete on who can come the furthest, the quickest, or the most copiously.

There are a number of reasons why men masturbate, the most obvious being the relief of sexual tension. Other reasons include to unwind from a stressful day, to provide a break in a particularly intense spate of concentration, to help sleep, or conversely to improve concentration.

Some men find that regular masturbation increases their sexual desire for their partners, while others find that they don't have enough for everyone, so they limit their private activities in order to save something for their partner.

CULTURAL DIFFERENCES

Some cultures and faiths believe that masturbation is unhealthy, disrespectful, or even sinful. If you've come from a background where there are strong opinions around the subject, you need to work out for yourself if these are beliefs you are happy to comply with or ones that do not fit with your worldview.

Choose a quickie or savor a longer, more sensual arousal

Women and masturbation

It often takes women longer to learn about self-pleasuring than men. A little girl sitting with legs apart, one hand up her skirt, is far more likely to reprimanded by a parent than is her brother who's got his hand deep in his trouser pocket. Discovering the sensations created by having your clitoris stroked often happens purely by chance. Some girls first experience this from sliding down the banisters, riding a bike, or sitting on the jet spray at the local swimming pool.

As little girls enter adolescence, they'll probably become more aware of genital arousal as they daydream and drool over their favorite celebrity or a boy at school. It's often then that they first use their hand to explore the sensation and perhaps fulfill it.

Women are more likely than men to use props to masturbate. Some people wrongly assume this indicates an aversion to touching their private parts, but it's more likely to be linked to the childhood memories of stimulation mentioned before, or simply a reflection of the fact that women learn to use props once a month anyway. The advent of the tampon encouraged women to feel much more comfortable inserting things into their vaginas, and consequently, discovering the wealth of delightful sensations stored within.

The reasons why women masturbate are largely the same as men, with the addition of using an orgasm to relieve period pain. Also, women are more likely than men to say that they masturbate for the sensual pleasure and not necessarily with the goal of achieving orgasm.

MASTURBATING IN FRONT OF YOUR PARTNER

Some couples find masturbating in their partner's presence highly erotic and the ultimate expression of trust and intimacy. Others want to curl up and die of embarrassment at the thought of it! There is no right and wrong, just different. Each couple must work out for themselves what feels right.

Getting to know you

The first step in learning how to stimulate your partner is to become familiar with the territory. As we've said before, men's bodies are usually less of a mystery to women, but remember that we are all created as unique individuals and no two of us are ever the same.

FOR THE GIRLS

Use a mirror if you feel uncomfortable with your partner examining you like a gynecologist. Prop it up on a pillow between your open legs and have your partner sit behind you, so that they can explore the reflection without increasing your sense of unease.

Getting to know your partner's body is essential for great sex

One of the difficulties in getting to know your partner's body is that it's not always convenient to look while you're actually touching. Generally, eye-to-eye contact is considered the most intimate and erotic. Therefore it's essential that you've had a good look round on a previous occasion and have imprinted a template of the terrain firmly into your brain.

One of the best and most fun ways of doing this is to play at being doctors and nurses, with or without the uniform.

Learning to enjoy touching and caressing your partner is one of the joys of lovemaking. It is also important to consider those areas that you wouldn't normally think of as being sexual, such as hands, arms, and feet. Be sensitive to your partner's responses and adjust your movements accordingly.

HOW TO PLAY DOCTORS AND NURSES

First of all you both need to agree that this is not a seductive prelude to sex. It's a time when you can both take it in turns to have a prod and a poke and really explore each other's body. If you both find the experience erotic and end up in the sack, then fine, but this should definitely not be your objective.

One of you needs to agree to be the patient while the other takes the role of medical practitioner. If you're the lucky one who's the doctor, then you can now begin the examination. Take your time and use this opportunity to ask all the questions that you could never ask in the middle of making love, such as, "Can you feel that?," "How far back does it go?," "What does it feel like if I bend it like this?" Remember to be gentle at all times. When you've finished your examination, swap roles.

If you feel completely totally ridiculous and collapse into fits of giggles, that's fine. It may seem utterly crazy at the time, but you'll be surprised how handy those bits of information will be in the future.

When you know the territory and have your basic orientation, it's time to finetune your stimulation skills. You'll find specific techniques on how to stimulate your partner in the coming pages, but first take some time to check out the next section on how to make sure your partner is enjoying your labors of love.

Show your partner that pleasing them pleases you

Are you nearly there yet?

When it comes to talking about technique, there are some approaches that are to be avoided at all costs. A lover who is impatient or gives the impression that your arousal or orgasm is a chore will be a total turn-off. The most important thing is to show your partner that pleasing them also pleases you.

The way to improve your technique is to ask for feedback while you're actually touching your partner. When giving oral, you'll have to stop for a moment before putting the question. Asking for feedback may sound very simple, but there are some essential guidelines to follow to ensure your questions are effective, and not intrusive.

Ask specific questions

What you really want to know is, "How good is this?" and the all important, "Is this good enough?"

Ask closed questions

These require one-word answers. While you're stimulating your partner, you want to help them to stay relaxed and focused on the sensations they are experiencing, not providing a philosophical response, during which time they may well have lost interest. Questions like, "Would you like me to be firmer or gentler?" are much better than, "What pressure would you like me to use?"

Use scaling questions

Ultimately feedback should tell you whether what you're doing increases or decreases arousal in your partner and brings them closer to, or further from orgasm. An effective way to achieve this is

---

HAND OVER HAND

Some couples find this technique really helpful for making sure they're in the right place and using the right motion and the right pressure. It doesn't really matter whose hand is on top, as long as the one doing the stimulating can feel what the other one is getting at. Combine this with asking for feedback.

to agree on a scaling system. For example, you might agree that on a scale of one to 10, one equals okay and 10 is orgasmic. When, let's say, your partner is on five, you could ask, "When I touch you like this, where are you?" If they respond with "Six," you know you're heading in the right direction. If they say "Four," you need to do something else.

When you first start asking for feedback it can feel as though you're barraging your partner with questions. But you will quickly learn the types of touch that your partner prefers and then you will just need to ask a few questions to clarify what they want at any particular time. Don't ever think that when you've learned it once, you've learned it for life. Our bodies are incredibly complex and what sends you off the orgasm scale on Saturday might only get you to level three the next day.

What turns you on may change from day-to-day

When talking about technique, do:	When talking about technique, don't:
Be encouraging	Become impatient
Be patient	Criticize
Show you're enjoying giving pleasure	Make comparisons with others
Ask specific, closed questions	Ask "Is this good?"
Use scaling questions	Ask "How much longer do you think you'll be?"
Give specific replies	Say "Oh don't bother I'll do it myself!"
Give honest replies	

Pleasing a woman

A lot of women prefer the gentler touch. This is, of course a huge generalization and you need to check it out with your partner, but it's always wiser to begin gently and become firmer. Going in with too heavy-handed an approach can be off-putting at best and downright painful at worst.

Whether the main focus of your attention is using your fingers or your tongue, you need to start slowly, building your partner's passion until she's ready to open up to you. Many try to go straight to the clitoris or vagina when it's just too early. Start by lovingly caressing her thighs, her belly, her buttocks, and her hips.

You'll know when she's really hotting up because she'll arch her back or open her legs and generally start undulating closer toward you. That's when you can begin to venture downward.

When you are between her legs, remember there are a lot of different things to play with. Remember to run your fingers through or gently tug her pubic hair. Caress her mons veneris and do a few circuits of the outer labia, before going in for the main attraction. Teasing, playful fingers or tongue are nearly always more popular than poking, grabbing ones.

The fine art of finger play

If you're continuing the journey with your fingers then you need to think about lubrication. Stimulating dry labia or a dry clitoris can be extremely uncomfortable and definitely not a turn-on. The female lubrication cells are all inside the vagina, so it could take some time before they're flowing freely enough to moisten the external area, so a little extra lube early on can be really beneficial. Remember to only use water-based lube if you're using condoms and remember that saliva is nature's ever-ready solution.

There are probably as many ways to stimulate a woman as there are women, so please don't think the following is by any means exhaustive. Here are some of the more popular basic moves, but the variations are endless.

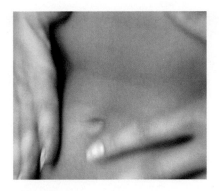

The labia tug

Some women find having their clitoris directly stimulated too sensitive. Many like the indirect stimulation that caressing or tugging the internal labia can create. One way to do this is to form your fingers into a "V" and rub them rhythmically up and down the sides of the clitoris inside the labia.

The clitoral circle

If your woman feels comfortable with direct clitoral stimulation, then another way is by putting the flat of your finger directly onto the clitoris and then making small circular movements. Some women prefer the sensation of two fingers with the clitoris nesting in the join, or three fingers where the middle one remains in contact with the clitoris while the other two caress around it. Remember to check what pressure your woman enjoys, and the circumference and direction of the circles.

The figure-of-eight

As above, one, two, or three fingers may be used but this time the figure-of-eight motion is utilized. The clitoris is stimulated at the crossover point. You circle the vulva and labia in one half of the eight, then circle the clitoris in the other, smaller half.

Plucking

Some women like the sensation of having their clitoris caressed backward and forward. This can best be achieved with one finger. Caress from the base close to the vagina and up toward the tip. Find out what pressure and tempo suits your lover best and continue as if plucking a beautiful melody.

Rolling

This is too sensitive for some women, but others love to have the clitoris rolled between finger and thumb. You can do this either with the skin of the labia covering or directly on the head of the clitoris.

Under the hood

Again, this is too much for some women. Make sure your lover is fully lubed and aroused. Basically any of the above motions can be used, but ensure that you are stimulating beneath the clitoral hood. You could either move this aside with your other hand or with a spare finger.

Fingering

Some women love to feel something inside them as their clitoris is being stimulated. Again this will vary from woman to woman and you need to be sure that she's ready to be penetrated. It's generally wiser to start with one finger up to the knuckle, and if that feels good, try a second, or even a third. Some women like a pumping in-and-out motion, while others prefer a circular motion, or even a combination of the two.

BOOB JOBS

Some women absolutely love having their breasts and nipples caressed—others don't particularly care. If your woman is the former, then make sure you take the time to discover the kind of touch she most enjoys.

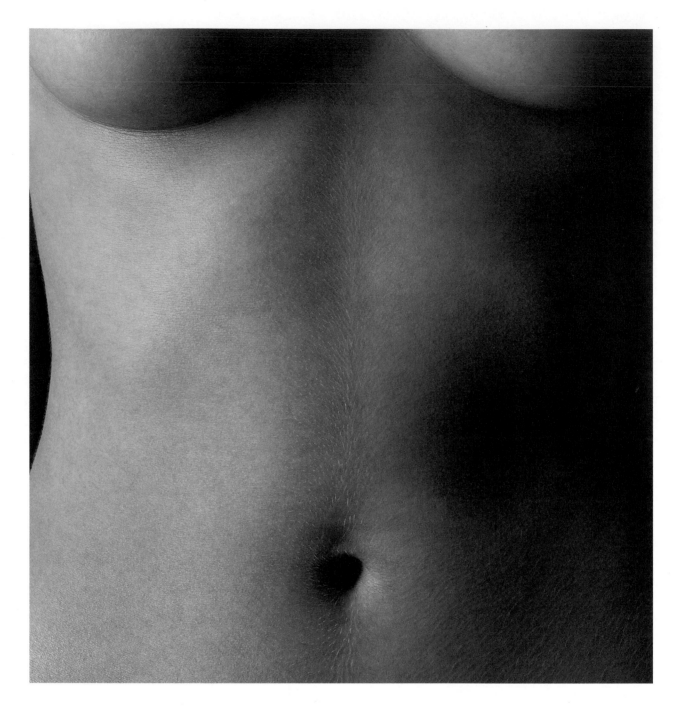

LUBRICATION

All women produce different amounts of lubrication, and this varies over the course of a month. Don't ever rely on wetness as your only guide to whether or not your partner is aroused—there could be times when she's dripping wet and uninterested, or dry and desperate.

Oral pleasure

Some women love oral sex, some hate it. Some men love giving it, some don't, it's simply a matter of personal preference. You need to remember the same basic principles as before of gradually, playfully, and teasingly making your way toward your lover's clitoris. Remember to prepare by kissing and licking her mons, her outer lips, inner lips, and round and round the clitoris, before approaching it directly.

The stimulation can be similar to the kinds described on the last page, but obviously using your tongue instead of your fingers. The circular motion, the figure-of-eight and plucking are most appropriate. Since the tongue is generally much softer (and wetter) than the fingers, you'll probably find your lover can enjoy more action directly on the clitoral head, but check that out first. You can also add the following techniques.

Flicking

You can use your tongue to flick up and down the clitoris. Some women prefer long, slow licks from the base of the shaft to the head, others prefer a feather-light speedy flick just on the head. Experimentation is always advisable.

Sucking

Gently sucking on the head of the clitoris and even drawing in some of the vulva as well can feel exquisite. Make sure you're gentle and release the vacuum gradually.

Oral sex has the great advantage of leaving you with two hands free. You can use one of those hands to splay your partner's lips open for easier access to the clitoris and reveal more from under the hood, while the other hand can be used to

Stubble rhythmically rubbed over the sensitive genital area really hurts! So either grow your beard or make sure you're clean-shaven beforehand

teasingly caress the vulva or vagina. Some women love the sensation of a fingertip inside the anus.

Remember that, however you're stimulating your partner, you need to enjoy it too. A woman who knows her man and is turned on by pleasing her will become even more turned on herself. So relax, enjoy what you're doing, and let her know it!

THE G-SPOT

A favorite way of stimulating the G-spot is to insert either one or two fingers in your lover's aroused vagina and make a "come here" motion with your fingers.

Pleasing
a man

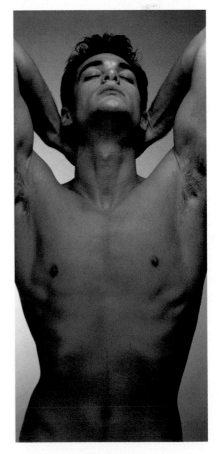

Probably the biggest complaint men have about women's touch is that it can often be too gentle. Perhaps because women tend to like a softer touch, they assume they should approach their man's member in the same way. But men are often made of tougher stuff and their penises will have received plenty of self-induced heavy-handedness.

Men tend to be less experimental than women when they masturbate, so often a partner can introduce them to a wider range of sensations then they thought possible.

The difference between mediocre and heavenly stimulation is often more about the attitude of the stimulator than the actual technique. A woman who seems reluctant, bored, or irritated by the activity can be a complete turn-off. The woman who is totally focused and obviously loving every minute of their partner's pleasure seems to be the fulfillment of every man's dream.

Men are sometimes happy to dispense with the preliminary warmups that many women enjoy before getting to the genitals, but they're missing a lot of additional pleasure, so don't rush. Take your time, no matter how much they beg, and tease and caress around the buttocks, the inner thighs, the lower belly, and pubic hair before meandering along the perineum toward the testes and the penis.

Hand-jobs

Most men agree that lubricated hand-jobs feel the best. With a little lube, the head of the penis will feel less sensitive and the hand can glide more smoothly up and down the shaft. However, sometimes there just isn't anything to hand (but remember that saliva can be a boon on such occasions). If you are stimulating dry, then you generally need to be more gentle and take more care around the tight frenulum area. There are many different ways of giving a man a hand-job and remember you'll need to ask him for feedback, to find out what pressure and stroke he's in the mood for. Here are some of the most popular movements.

Twister

Pump

This is the basic up-and-down motion, but there are variations. Whatever way you do it you need to be sure that your movements are smooth, fluid, and continuous. You can either do it with one hand gripped around the penis and with all five fingers in contact, or just make a ring with two or three. There is a huge difference in sensation, depending on the length of stroke and the position of the hands. Some men love to have the thumb or fingertips positioned so they caress the frenulum with each stroke, while for others this is too sensitive. Check it out with your man.

Two-handed pump

One stays gripped around the base, while the other pumps up and down as required.

Two-hand shuffle

Both hands, one after the other, stroke the penis in an upward direction only. Keep the movement continuous so as one hand leaves the top of the penis the other is already following close behind.

Twister

There are two ways of doing this. Both require a twisting motion with your hand:

Version one is to work your hand all the way from the base of the shaft to the glands, but using a twisting motion as you go. The other is focused on the sensitive glands and frenulum and requires the use of just two fingers, twisting as if you were taking the top off a bottle.

CIRCUMCISION

Circumcised men may have a glans that can cope with rougher handling while their uncircumcised friend prefers the protection of his foreskin when stimulated. Unless of course, you have tons of lube and a tender touch.

Whatever you do, watch your teeth

Blow jobs

In general, the principles are the same as those used for hand-jobs, as described on the last page. Make sure you start slow and teasingly. Kissing and licking his belly and inner thighs, then working toward his perineum, balls, and finally, before he bursts with anticipation, his penis. And whatever you're doing, watch your teeth!

Pumping

With your neck and throat relaxed, and your lips forming an "O" firmly around his shaft, take as much of his penis in your mouth as you can and move up and down, starting slowly and then building faster. This is sometimes known as "deep throat" after the classic 1970s porn movie of the same name. Some men prefer for their partner to work just on the head of the penis, so using the "O" shape as before, focusing all attention on stroking the sensitive glans.

With hand

Whether you're deep-throating or

TESTICLE TEASING

Whether you're giving a hand- or blow-job, don't forget to include a little testicular teasing. Some men love to have their balls cradled and gently massaged, or you could experiment with giving them a little suck. Remember to be gentle, and check out which are the best moves.

concentrating just on the head, some men love to feel your hand on the lower part of their penis as well. Some prefer for you to just continue firm pressure around the base, while others will love it if you allow your well-lubricated hand to follow the motion of your mouth.

Tongue massage
Either while you're pumping, or as a separate action altogether, use your tongue to caress the sensitive frenulum. You can do this either with the flat of your tongue, the tip of your tongue, or the back of your tongue. Ask your man which he prefers. Another way to use your tongue is to massage round and round the head of the glans in firm, smooth, rhythmical circles.

Humming
Some men absolutely love this while others find it unbearably ticklish. While your man's penis is in your mouth, begin to hum or moan. They will feel the sensation reverberate through to their penis and go mad, either with delight or with giggles!

Whatever technique you use to please your man, make sure you keep asking for feedback, keep learning, keep experimenting, and most importantly, keep having fun.

ANAL STIMULATION

For many men, the prostate is a delightful bundle of erotic nerves that adds extra depth to their orgasm when stimulated. You can either do this by inserting a well-lubricated finger inside their anus and making small gentle massage strokes, or some men feel more comfortable if you massage around the rim of the anus or indirectly by applying pressure through the perineum.

Penetrative sex

Penetrative sex is physically the closest any of us will ever be to another human being. Your bodies merge and become one which is why, for many people, it is a mystical union. Here we explore some of the joys and myths of intercourse, and offer practical information and advice.

Joys and myths

Intercourse is the sexual act that allows our bodies to merge into a single, synchronous, mutually pleasurable unit. For many humans, it seems instinctive to seek penetration. Men yearn to be engulfed and women long to be filled. But it is not the be all and end all of great sex.

Many people still refer to intercourse as "real sex" and consider the rest as foreplay. They might love sensual massage and relish oral sex, but are always waiting for the grand finale—penetration. This thinking has two major flaws.

Firstly, it relegates other, perfectly beautiful sexual activities to second place and thereby robs them of all of their pleasure.

Secondly, it assumes that couples who don't have intercourse for physical reasons—and, in particular, the high percentage of the gay population who don't practice penetration—are second-class sexual citizens.

Another problem with believing that intercourse is the most important element of sex is that it becomes the thing you do at the end of the sexual experience. So often, men feel that they should wait for penetration before they come, and when they have, the encounter is over. Yet more than 50% of women don't reach orgasm through penetration because there isn't sufficient stimulation of the clitoris. This means they must either have their orgasm first, or go without! Great sex means you can move from intercourse, to oral, to manual, and back again, in any order and as many times as you wish.

One of the great joys of intercourse is that you can both stimulate each other simultaneously. But here lies another potentially dangerous expectation. Just because you can both be stimulated at the same time doesn't mean that you'll both be aroused at the same rate. Nor does it mean that you'll both be receiving the optimum stimulation required for orgasm.

Some years ago, the mutual orgasm became almost the Holy Grail of great sex. But in reality, striving for perfectly synchronized, mutually satisfying sex is like trying to scratch your head and rub your stomach at the same time. Concentrating on giving your partner pleasure will often mean that you're distracted from your own, so the orgasm you experience may be weaker. What's more, it also means you're not fully available to share your

Great sex means you can move from intercourse, to oral, to manual, and back again, in any order and as many times as you wish

partner's rising rapture and their orgasm—in other words, the worst of both worlds.

Great lovers recognize the point when either their own or their partner's orgasm is imminent, and then take it in turns to let their body be used.

Anal penetration

Some people think anal sex is the ultimate in liberated sexual pleasure while others consider it distasteful.

Many couples are happy to experiment and find out for themselves. If they both like it, they'll continue with it. If only one of them likes it and the other doesn't mind doing the honors, then one of them will continue. But some may find it too uncomfortable and decide never to venture there again.

The rectum is full of sensitive nerve-endings. The male prostate is highly sensitive and the nerve pathway from the penis to the brain runs through the rectum. Men can also enjoy penetrating a women's rectum because it provides a snugger, more stimulating, fit than the vagina. Some women have powerful orgasms when the anus is stimulated, particularly the wall between the vagina and the anus.

The difference between anal ecstasy and anal agony is relaxation. To enjoy anal sex, you need to work on relaxing the sphincter muscle. Scrupulous hygiene is also essential. To prevent transmission of STDs use the anal-grade heavy-duty condoms designed for the purpose.

The difference between anal ecstasy and anal agony is relaxation

Coital harmony

On the basis that sex is a natural human instinct, you'd think there wouldn't be a lot to say about you and your lover being in synch and ready to roll. But there are many aspects to consider before you experiment with different sexual positions.

Body ratios

Some couples fit together very easily. But many don't. Guidance on sexual positions often assumes the former, and can leave couples wondering why they can't achieve even the simplest physical maneuver. The reason is that most of us are different shapes and sizes, unlike the perfectly anatomically matched couple in illustrations and photographs on this subject.

If your partner is 6ft 2in and you're 5ft 4in, some positions will be impossible. If your partner has, shall we say, a generous waistline, and your arms are normal length, the "perfect position for simultaneous manual stimulation" might be completely lost on you.

Another important aspect of body ratios is the size of a man's penis. If it is of average size (five or six inches when erect) then you and your partner can probably enjoy most positions. But as some well-endowed men have discovered, contrary to the media hype, their partner does not swoon with delight at their approaching member, but sometimes recoils in horror. The positions that allow for deeper penetration may be the very ones you have to avoid.

As a couple, you will soon discover the positions that work best for you, but please don't think that just because it looks good on the picture or promises a certain type of stimulation, that it will work for you. Some of us are just not made that way.

Being ready

It is essential that both of you are ready for penetration, both emotionally and physically. In many faiths and cultures, the act of penetration has particular significance and therefore while you may be ready for other forms of sexual intimacy, you may not feel ready for intercourse.

It's also important that you are both ready physically. Most people know that, without at least a partial erection, penetration is impossible for a man. But you also need to be sure that the women's body is ready too.

PRACTICING NEW POSITIONS

Some sexual positions will stretch you to the limit of your physical capabilities, while others just won't work because of your body ratios. To avoid wrecking a passionate moment because a limb gives way or gets cramp, practice new positions with your clothes on. Set an evening aside and experiment to your heart's content. Try some of the more demanding positions and see how your bodies fit together. And while you're there, see how long you can really hold it for! If you collapse, you can guarantee it will be in a fit of laughter rather than frustration.

FANNY FARTS

The movement of a penis in and out of a vagina often causes air to get trapped—and when it's released, it sounds like a fart.

When this happens, no apologies are required since both of you did it!

Experiment with different speeds. Hard and fast is not always best

Docking procedures

Rarely discussed because there's an assumption that "getting it in" is easy, a significant number of couples wonder whether they should really be poking around until they manage to dock without any manual intervention. And if they do need a hand who's hand should it be?

Women may feel particularly nervous asking a man if they'd like a guiding hand, fearing they will cause offense by implying their partner is incompetent. Some men may feel that using their own hand represents failure. But the penis is not fitted with a homing device! And, depending on the position, the entrance to a women's vagina is not always at the right angle. If you want to enjoy a variety of sexual positions, then as a couple you'll need to negotiate around this little issue of etiquette. Otherwise, both of you will miss out.

Thrusting issues

Hard and fast is not always best. Shallow thrusting allows the sensitive head of the penis to be in contact with the sensitive lower third of the vagina. The lower third of the vagina is also tighter, and it can feel wonderful for both to feel the wider part of the coronal ridge against this area. Deeper thrusting allows the whole of the shaft of the penis to be caressed and the woman may also be able to benefit from having her clitoris caressed by the male pubic bone. The labia also tend to get pulled more which can be an indirect way of caressing the clitoris.

Fast thrusting is often associated with frenzied passion, whether it's deep or shallow, while slow thrusting can seem more sensuous and more teasing. Both can feel amazing and of course, there's no reason why you can't mix-and-match. It really is a case of different strokes for different folks. Whatever position you find yourselves in, make sure you experiment and check what feels good for each other.

BEING EXPELLED

Sometimes, the strength of contractions a woman experiences on orgasm force the man's penis out of her vagina. The general advice most women give if that happens is to re-enter swiftly.

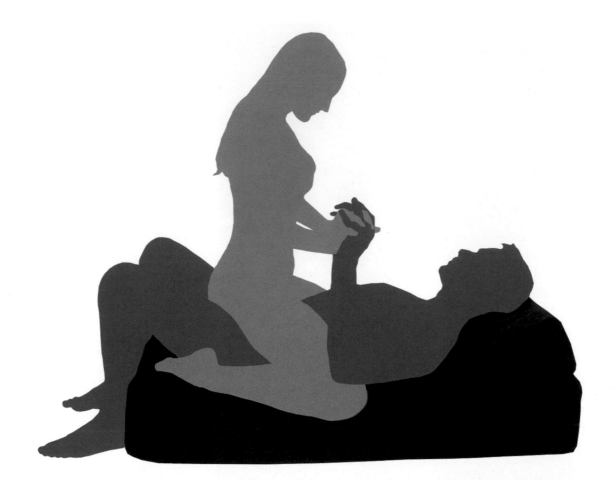

Sexual positions

It has been calculated that more than 600 different sexual positions involve penetration. Not all are widely different and there's no doubt that you would both need to be Olympic gymnasts to achieve some of them. Analysis of these demonstrates that they revolve around four basic positions.

Man on top

The most popular and most regularly used. With the man on top, a couple can maintain good eye contact, body ratios allowing, and the man has overall control of the thrusting motion.

The key variations on this position are:

When the women raises her legs, penetration will be deeper. If the man also rides high as in this illustration, and uses a rocking rather than thrusting motion, his pubic bone will give additional stimulation to the clitoris.

With legs fully extended and hooked over his shoulders. This allows for deep penetration and if her arms are long enough she can also caress his testes or prostate. Her hands are also free to hold his hips and indicate the rhythm and depth of thrust she would like.

If you have any back or joint complaints, be careful when trying new positions. If in doubt, check with your doctor

More man on top

This position is known as "splitting the bamboo," allowing more pressure to be applied to one side of the vagina. The raised leg can be used as leverage for either individual.

In this kneeling position, the man does not need to be overly concerned about supporting his body weight. This means both hands are free to stimulate either her breasts or clitoris, or both.

This can also work well if the man is standing. You'll need to make sure the woman's body is raised to an appropriate height. The kitchen table could be ideal.

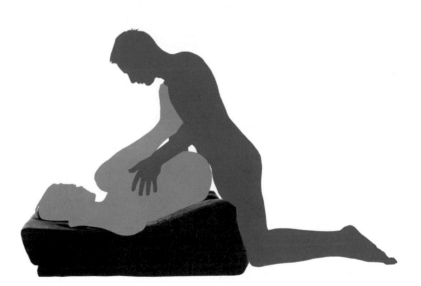

SEX IN DIFFERENT PLACES

Don't forget to vary where and when you make love. Leaving sex for in bed at night will soon get monotonous. Let any time of day be a good time for sex and enjoy making love al fresco, in front of the fire, in the conservatory looking up at the night sky—any time, any place, anywhere.

Woman on top

In this position the woman has maximum control of thrusting. She can choose deep or shallow, or rock or grind against the male pubic bone to stimulate her clitoris. It's the perfect position in which to tease the man.

Men also enjoy this position because they can lie back and enjoy the view. Rather than taking the usual leading role, then can enjoy watching their partner take the reins.

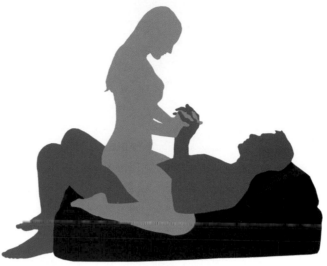

The 45–degree angle in this picture is best for deep penetration. If the woman were to lie forward—or back (though do this with great care, as it can hurt the penis) then the sensation would be very different.

This shows how the man can also change position to vary sensation, allowing him to have a little more control over thrusting.

With the woman facing away from her partner, she can move backward and forward very easily and can also stimulate herself by hand if she wants. Many men are turned on by buttocks, so this position gives them an unparalleled view.

Side-by-side

A favorite among those who love to be alongside each other, sharing the responsibility for thrusting. It also allows for maximum body contact and both of you have your hands free for caressing. A popular variation of this is "spoons." This is when the man lies behind the woman with the front of his body touching her back and enters the vagina from behind.

From behind

This position, often referred to as "doggy style" is one of the best for stimulating the G-spot, since the penis comes from a different angle and stimulates the front vaginal wall where the G-spot lies.

This is the basic position, though she could be on all fours. This requires that body ratios are relatively well-matched.

The man doesn't have to support his weight and both can lean backward or forward as necessary to change the angle. You can also have a nice back rub too, though breasts or clitoris might be preferred.

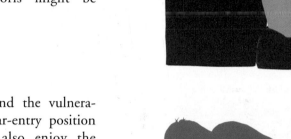

Women may find the vulnerability of the rear-entry position exciting. Men also enjoy the dominance that this position gives them.

For maximum penetration and optimum angle, penetrate with the man standing and the woman bending over. Again, this leaves hands free for extra stimulation. Whilst this position looks like hard work for the woman, the combination of vaginal, G-spot, breast, and clitoral stimulation make it well worth the effort.

Many thanks to Loving-angles (Angles Global Ltd)® who provided the images for this section. Angles are a range of foam-covered shapes designed specifically to enhance sexual pleasure. For more details go to: www.loving-angles.com™

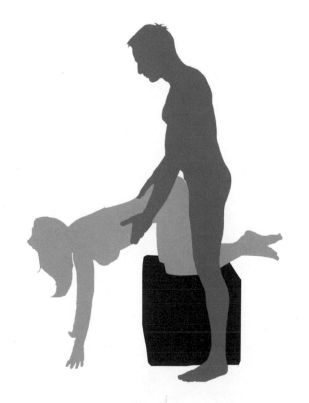

The raunchy stuff

Many couples enjoy raunchy stuff, a bit of extra excitement. As well as being intimate and loving, sex should be fun and exciting. Injecting games into a sexual relationship can add a new dimension and ensure that lovemaking doesn't become boring.

Let's play

Many adults have serious problems adapting to play during sex, associating it with immaturity. Some believe sex should only be erotic and steamy, not playful, and thus silly. Being silly was frowned up on when we were children, and the fact that play is about becoming more child-like and vulnerable increases anxiety among certain adults. You may feel a little inhibited at first, but give it a try—you'll find it fun!

A reason many people give for not playing games is that they can't see the point. If this describes you or your partner, then my suggestion would be to give it a try and find out for yourself. You may feel a little inhibited at first, but once you get into the swing, I guarantee you'll love it.

The choice is limitless, but here are a few ideas you might like to try.

Sex games

There are many ways of sexing up your normal activities. Performing any daily routine in the nude is going to make it far more interesting, whether you are reconciling your checkbook, washing the dishes, or cooking the evening meal.

You can also add sexy twists to old favorites, for example, hide-and-seek. You hide an object somewhere around the house and attached to it are details of a sexual favor that you'll perform if the object is found.

A blindfold can be used for a range of sensual games. Blindfold your partner and give them objects to feel and identify. Choose items that have sexual connotations and add the occasional real, live body part. Losing the sense of sight often heightens other senses, so it can be particularly exciting to blindfold your partner and then tease their body with different textures.

You can also "sex up" some of the standard commercial games that you already have in the home. Everyone's heard of strip poker, but any game can involve removing an item of clothing as the penalty for losing. You could also try a game of Scrabble where every word has to be rude, or Pictionary or Taboo, in which the word you're trying to describe has sexual connotations.

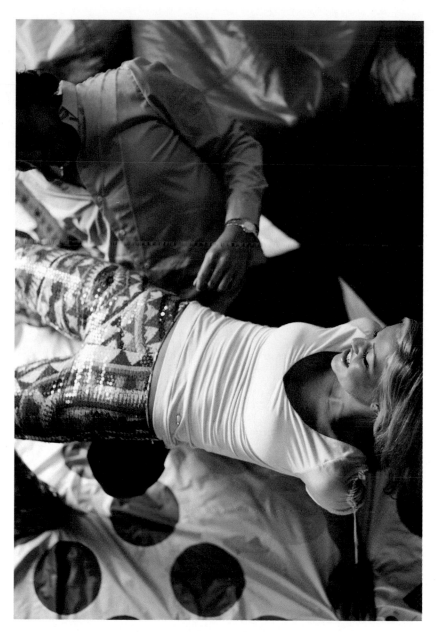

Hours of fun can be obtained from a simple pair of dice. Write a list of sexual activities that relate to certain throw combinations. For example, rolling a three might be a kiss, a four a genital fondle, and nine oral sex. Reserve the double six for something really special.

Alternatively, assign one to six on one die with different body parts and one to six on the other with different types of touch—stroke, kiss, lick, tweak. Roll the dice and follow the instructions.

A range of commercial sex games are available to be enjoyed with your partner. Try a game of Sexual Pursuits, Romantic Dares, Caught In The Act, Kama Sutra, The Game, Lust, Nookii – the list is endless. And so can be the fun.

PLAY FIGHTS

Play fights are not just for kids. Getting your adrenalin going with a friendly tussle will not only get your heart beating faster but it will also leave your body more responsive and easily aroused.

Remember that wet play is slippery, so be extra-careful when trying an adventurous position

Water fun

Lathering each other up in the bathtub or shower can provide bountiful pleasure. The silky sensation of water and bath oils can make the skin feel beautifully sensual. Whether you're in the tub or shower, spend some time soaping each other, then rinsing each other down with the showerhead. If you've got a pulse option on it, you may find this particularly invigorating.

A range of bath products specifically designed for lovers is now available. Try some passion fruit bubble bath. When you've finished in the tub, be sure to continue to pamper each other's senses. A wide range of lotions and oils can be used to slowly and seductively condition your partner's skin.

Dressing up

Many men and women enjoy the sensual touch of satin, silk, lace, or leather next to their skin. Lots of lingerie is available for both sexes to enjoy. Whether you prefer something feminine, something sophisticated, or something raunchy, you're bound to find a garment you like.

Many couples also enjoy dressing up for role-play. You might fancy a game of Doctors and Nurses, Chambermaid, Serving Wench, or Stripper. The clothes might not stay on for long or you might like to work your way around them.

Some people simply enjoy wearing the clothes while others like to get fully into the role and build a sexual scenario around them, to act out over the course of the night.

STRIPPING

Many couples enjoy teasing each other with their own personal strip show. The art of a good strip is based on slow, deliberate movements. Slip into something sexy, put on some music, and slowly and sensually take each item off, one at a time. Remember to let your partner see how much what you're doing is turning you on too.

Enjoying Erotica

What is erotic or pornographic is purely subjective. The range of erotica nowadays is much wider than the tawdry under-the-counter magazines of the past. In addition, anything that you read or see that "turns you on" is erotic. It might be romantic or sensual with a mere hint of something sexual.

Many aspects of sex—arousal, fantasy, physical stimulation, and masturbation—are enhanced by the reading of erotica and viewing pornographic material, whether on your own or with your partner.

The key to enjoyment is that you reach the comfort zone, a place in which the degree and content of material is acceptable to both parties.

If you feel a little uncomfortable with the idea of introducing erotica into your relationship, then start with material that is light in tone. In fact, start by reading this chapter together and discuss what you think of the notion, and what type of erotica turns you on.

When you have both accepted that this can be an effective means of enhancing your sex lives, move on to something a little more raunchy. Always remember that the experience won't be truly erotic unless you're both obtaining enjoyment from it. If one of you is only going along with it to placate the other's desires, neither of you will truly benefit because at least one of you will feel unfulfilled. So make sure you're open and honest with each other about how each experience affects you.

Erotic literature

Erotic literature has been booming for several years. While your local bookshop will almost certainly have copies of Nancy Friday's pioneering trilogy *My Secret Garden, Forbidden Flowers*, and *Women on Top* —all of which provide compilations of real-life sexual fantasies—there are also many classic novels, including *Hot Gossip* by Savannah Smythe, *Dream Story* by Arthur Schnitzler, and *The Story Of O* by Pauline Réage. All these books are popular and readily available

and are complemented by the short stories that appear in such magazines as the subscription-based *Erotic Review*, which describes itself as being aimed at the primary sexual organ—the brain. Another is *The Hot Spot*, produced six times a year. It contains regular selections of short stories aimed at the female reader as well as real-life confessions and fantasies.

Magazines

Such publications as the *Erotic Review* and *The Hot Spot* provide tasteful illustrations and erotic fact and fiction. Outside of the internet, the more glossy mainstream magazines are still the most easily accessible form of erotic material, with ever-increasing in range and diversity.

Start with magazines such as *Cosmopolitan* or those for guys such as *FHM*. If your requirements are for something stronger and more risqué yet still tasteful, go for *Penthouse, Playboy,* and *Playgirl*, or the longstanding *Forum*, containing

It won't be erotic unless you're both enjoying it

erotic fiction, letters, and interviews.

The boundaries of subject matter appear limitless. Titles such as *Horny Housewives*, are available at convenience stores, but if you feel uncomfortable about buying these from retail outlets then the internet provides the perfect opportunity to purchase and subscribe discreetly.

On–screen sex

Many couples enjoy watching erotic movies together. Again, the choice is vast, ranging from mildly titillating and deeply romantic, through soft porn to fullon, hardcore movies. A visit to your local video rental store will provide you with an idea of what there is to choose from. You might fancy a high-school romp such as *American Pie*, with its humorous take on the subject, the very British raunchiness of the *Carry On* series of movies, or their spiritual successors, the Austin Powers movies.

There's plenty covering the more heartfelt aspects in the romance section, such as *The Piano* or *Pride & Prejudice*, and excellent erotic thrillers such as *Secretary*. The 18-and-over section contains thrillers with overtly erotic content such as *Eyes Wide Shut*, or historic movies such as *Les Liaisons Dangereuses*. Then there are the mostly plotless but graphic adult movies. If you enjoy adult-only movies but run out of choices at your local store, the internet provides many online opportunities.

In these post-feminist times many companies target couples who view erotic movies together. For instance, *Hot Rod's Blue* range is intended not only for couples but also for women,

reflected in the emphasis on storylines and strong female characters.

Art

Since the dawn of history, erotic subject-matter has been depicted in art. The naked human form has been the subject of enduring fascination, from cave-drawings through Picasso, via hundreds of artists such as Gustav Klimt, Egon Schiele, and Paul Gaugin. Much contemporary erotic art is subtle and discreet, but it can also be graphic, funny, or simply beautiful.

Photography is probably the best medium for erotic imagery, whether through the *noir* lens of such photographers as Tony Ward, Paul Freeman, and the late Helmut Newton, or the nitty-gritty approach of the likes of Richard Kern and Terry Richardson.

Meanwhile, the Japanese comic-book style of Hentai—in which the females are doe-eyed, big-breasted, and youthful with pale skin—is considered by millions to be sexy, judging by the huge market for it around the world.

Probably the best place to begin to explore erotic art—as well as what turns you on—is by logging on to The Erotic Print Society website at www.eroticprints.org.

Watching an erotic movie can give a couple new ideas to spice up their sex life

---

BECOME A MOVIE CRITIC

Get yourself a little black book and set up your very own erotic movie review. Rent out a range of movies over the next few weeks, and score them on different criteria, such as production values, storyline, acting ability, explicitness, credibility, sexiness of the cast, and of course, arousability. Add whatever comments you think necessary. Compare grades and comments at the end of period and nominate your top 10.

Playful products

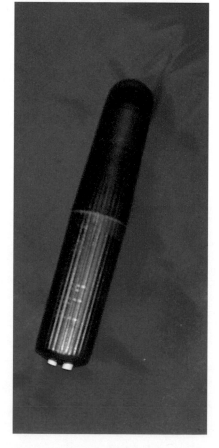

To attain maximum enjoyment out of playing together toys are a necessity. The choice is vast and with the internet you don't even have to leave home to buy. You might want to purchase your lover a little gift to remind them of you during the day or something that you can share together at night.

Novelty items

Starting with the edible novelties, there are chocolate dicks and edible panties. You can also have fun with chocolate body paint, or just plain old chocolate spread! Half the fun (for the recipient, anyway) is in the application, so invest in a brush and stroke it on before licking and sucking it off. A slight variation on this theme is body-decorating kits that are a little like cake-decorating kits. They include gels and pastes of different colors and flavors, along with applicators, so after decorating you partner you can admire your artwork before destroying it with your mouth.

Lubes and lotions

Not only is good lubrication essential to stop sex being painful, it can also increase the sensual experience of touch. You can now buy standard lubes such KY Jelly from your local drugstore or supermarket. If you want something a little different, plenty of variety is available from specialist stores and websites. Many of the products are also designed to taste good as well as feel great.

Most water-based lubricants will be labeled as being suitable for use with condoms, whereas other oils (including massage oils) and oil based "novelty" lubricants would cause the rubber to erode and split, so bear this in mind when you're choosing.

Vibrators

Vibrators are by far the most popular sex toy.

Once upon a time, the only "personal massagers" as they were euphemistically known, were cumbersome and looked a bit like a flatbed sander! Nowadays, the choice of size and shape is quite bewildering.

The traditional penis shape is still very popular but there are also vibrators in shapes specifically for stimulating the clitoris, G-spot and general vulval region. You can buy vibrators big enough to intimidate the best-hung man in America, and one small enough to slip into your pocket. Many are cleverly disguised so you can leave them on your bedside table.

The materials used to make vibrators has also changed and expanded. Smoother, softer plastics that feel more like flesh now overshadow the old clinical plastic or cold metal ones. There is also a choice of how you get your buzz. Choose batteries, mains-powered, or rechargeable. There are remote-controlled devices and the buzz can be quiet and gentle, or loud and vigorous. And don't forget the two-speed models and vibrators that are pre-programmed to give the optimum range of vibrations.

If you've never used a vibrator my advice is to get one today. Start off with a simple model and see how it feels, then build up your collection as the fancy takes you.

Many men really enjoy the

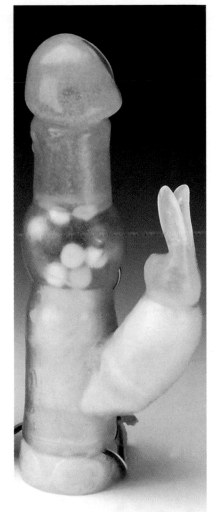

sensations of a vibrator too. Start on the slowest speed and tease around the perenium, testes, and base of penis before moving toward the highly sensitive head.

MORE THAN A TOY

Vibrators have been used in psychosexual therapy for many years. Clinical research has been undertaken that proves that, in the majority of cases, vibrators can improve orgasmic response in both men and women. When vibratory stimulation is applied to the clitoris or shaft of the penis, the glandipudendal (bulbocavernosus) reflex is strengthened. It is this reflex that is responsible for orgasm. Vibrators need to work at between 70–100 revs per second and oscillate no more than 2.4mm, but they do not need to be penis-shaped. It is not uncommon for individuals who have never had an orgasm to use vibratory stimulation for up to an hour, three times a week for a number of weeks, before the muscles are sufficiently toned to respond.

The Hot stuff

Sex can be enjoyable, whether it's tender and romantic or playful and passionate. But some days you want it hot, raw, and intense. Here we introduce you to some of the lesser-known sex toys and explore the world of fetish, fantasy, bondage, and S&M.

More sex toys

In addition to vibrators, there is a huge range of toys designed to spice up your sex life and add extra stimulation. These include love-balls, strap-ons, ticklers, butt plugs, artificial vaginas, and dildos, some of which can even be molded to perfectly match your partner's penis.

Love-balls

There are quite a range of these but the basic model comprises two weighted balls, each about 1¼ inches in diameter. Slip them into your vagina. As you walk, the balls will rock and roll, providing a lovely sensation. They also help strengthen the pelvic floor muscles.

Ticklers

These attachments for the penis provide extra stimulation of the clitoris on penetration and are available in a variety of materials. A variation on this is the Tassled Cock Ring that gently caresses the testes and the perineum as it swings. Another option is a clitoris finger stimulator (pictured right).

Dildos

Penis-shaped objects have been around for at least 30,000 years. These days they come in a range of shapes, sizes, and textures from smooth cylindrical shapes to those designed to look like a real penis, complete with testes. If you want one to perfectly match your partner's physique, you can buy a molding kit and make your own. Passion8 sell a kit that includes everything you need to make a mold of your partner's penis. Once made, this mold can be sent off and filled with anything from plastic to marble to solid gold (funds permitting of course!).

Strap-ons

A number of dildos are available with a special harness known as a strap-on. The harness can be worn by either a man or a woman to penetrate the other partner. Many women enjoy playing the role of penetrator, either with a female partner or to anally stimulate a man. There are also double strap-ons that stimulate vaginally and

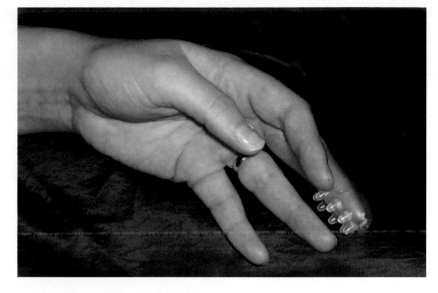

anally together, and double-ended strap-ons that stimulate the wearer and partner simultaneously.

Butt plugs

There are a number of toys specifically designed for providing anal stimulation. In addition to vibrators and dildos, the butt plug has been designed to insert into the anus to give a feeling of fullness. They come in different sizes and shapes but all have a flanged end to ensure they don't get lost!

Artificial vaginas

The blow-up doll is still with us and is now a much better crafted toy than ever before. New materials have made the sensation even more lifelike. If you fancy something with a little more "buzz," you can invest in a vibrating vagina.

A strap-on harness can be worn by either a man or a woman to penetrate the other partner

HEALTH & SAFETY

It's essential that sex toys are thoroughly cleaned after use and there are now products specifically made for the purpose. You should also remember never to insert anything from anus to vagina without thoroughly cleaning it first as this can cause infection.

If you're going to insert something, make sure it's been specifically designed for the job. Not only is getting a foreign object stuck in an orifice embarrassing, it may also be extremely painful and dangerous.

Bondage and S&M

Bondage and S&M are not the same thing—or at least not necessarily. Bondage does not have to include anything painful whereas S&M does. S&M almost always includes an element of bondage, however. Try using silk scarves, ropes, handcuffs, and whips or just spank with your hand.

There are a range of different sorts of practices that fall under the general headings of bondage and S&M, beginning with a gentle spank or light restraint, through bondage chambers and whips. If you're not sure what you think you'd enjoy, it's always best to start at the light side and slowly expand your repertoire.

Light bondage

Light bondage is enjoyed by many couples and regularly practiced in bedrooms around the world. It includes light restraint and gentle spanking.

Many people enjoy being restrained during sex play. Having your hands tied behind your back or tied to the bedposts forces you to be totally passive. It takes away any responsibility for giving pleasure to your partner, so you can simply lie back and receive. For many, this sense of passivity is highly erotic, but for others it can feel scary and/or frustrating. For the person who is doing the tying down, the feelings of control and power can be delicious. You can tease and caress until your partner begs you to stop. Or use their body for your own pleasure.

Taking it in turns to be tied down will give you both the chance to see how it feels in each role. Make sure that if either of you begins to feel uncomfortable at any stage, you stop.

A little light spanking can increase arousal for a number of reasons. The first is that the anticipation builds adrenalin. And adrenalin heightens the body's responsiveness to stimulation. Endorphins, one of nature's feelgood chemicals and pain-relievers, are also released by sexual activity. It is believed that this double release makes the combination of pain and sex especially enjoyable. Finally, a

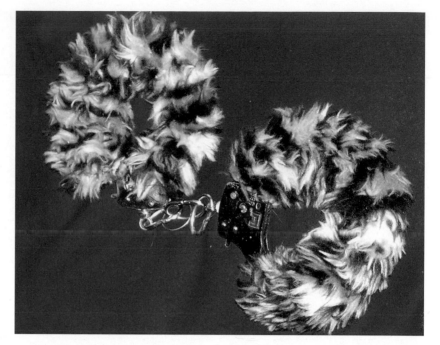

succession of smacks on the rump will send reverberating vibrations through the genital organs, so as long as there isn't too much of a sting to distract you, you'll be getting stimulated in more places than the obvious one. If you fancy trying light bondage, you might like to invest in a few accessories.

Light accessories

There are plenty of items around the home that you can use to tie each other up, such as scarves and neckties, but be aware that they can knot very tightly indeed if you pull on them.

Alternatively you can buy some Love Cuffs, trimmed with fake fur, or some heavier-duty handcuffs and ankle cuffs. These have the advantage of being easily removable—as long as you don't lose the key of course.

For spanking, you can obviously use your hand, which has the advantage of the smacker also being able to feel how hard the smack is. Or you could use pretty much anything else around the house. If you want a bit of extra realism, you can buy a whip.

Whatever you do, make sure

smacking starts gently and builds up slowly. Forgetting your own strength and giving a painful wallop is a real passion-wrecker.

Having your hands tied to the bedposts forces you to be totally passive

CONSENT
Bondage and S&M are only erotic when practiced by two consenting people. It involves a high level of trust and absolute faith that one partner will stop if the other feels uncomfortable.

Heavy bondage and S&M

This is where the chains, leather, and heavy-duty whips come in. Heavy bondage has a big cult following and there are many magazines, videos, stores, and clubs dedicated to the subject. The term heavy bondage is usually used to include the practices of S&M, D&S, and B&D. For those of you not on the scene:

S&M – Sado-masochism

One person plays the sadist (someone who enjoys inflicting pain) and one person plays the masochist (someone who enjoys receiving pain). Some people prefer to always play the same role while others swap round.

D&S – Dominance & Submission

Akin to S&M, but pain doesn't have to be involved. The person who is Dominant, often referred to as the "Top" or "Dom," gives orders and commands to the person who is submissive, called the "Bottom" or "Sub." This slave-and-master-type role-play with sexual commands usually involves wearing rubber or leather. Some prefer always to play the same role while others try both.

B&D – Bondage & Discipline

One person is tied up, humiliated, physically punished and disciplined. Sex industry workers earn particularly high sums for offering these sorts of services.

People who are into heavy bondage enjoy the rituals associated with the scene as much as the sexual stimulation. Although many of us can't understand how pain and humiliation can be enjoyable, heavy bondage practitioners seem to process and experience their encounters in a different way.

They may have as intimate and stimulating an experience as any other type of sexual encounter. In fact for them, it is more so. The scene also has its own range of equipment.

Heavy equipment

As well as the "light" equipment you might decide that it's time to get some extras. In addition to the standard handcuffs and ankle cuffs you might also want some harnesses and even a bondage chair or bed.

Whips or canes can be used to inflict pain or punishment. For a change from the sting of a whip or cane, you could buy a paddle to provide more of a dull thud. You can also buy a range of clamps for attaching to different parts of the body.

If you're into submission, purchase a collar and chain restraint kit or a specifically designed penis restraint.

Couples interested in the heavy bondage scene should proceed slowly and with caution. Keep checking that both of you are still enjoying what you're doing and that both of you are ready to move on. If you find you're running out of choices at your local store, the internet provides enormous opportunities to rent or buy online.

SAYING NO

Experts in S&M never say no. Or rather, they say no a lot of the time but no-one pays any attention, since "No, No, please, more!" just adds to the fun of the game. That is why serious practitioners have developed their own universally understood vocabulary.

Saying "Yellow" means "slow down a bit, not quite so hard, let up a bit."

Saying "Red" means "stop now." You and your partner could agree to using these terms if you like, or think up something else. What's important is that you both know how to say "no" and mean it.

Fetishes

What makes something a fetish rather than simply additional stimulation depends on how important the object of the fetish is for sexual arousal. If you're turned on by high heels or the feel of rubber, and enjoy sometimes incorporating them into your sex life—that's a matter of taste. However, if you can't get turned on *without* a pair of high heels or rubber, or you spend a lot of your waking hours thinking about the particular objects of your desire, this is a fetish.

A fetish is not a problem, as long as your partner understands and enjoys it as well. And if you can find someone who shares your fetish, even better. But for some couples, a fetish can cause serious problems. When one person becomes reliant on a particular prop, body part, or scenario in order to get aroused, the partner can feel as if they come in second place to the fetish. They might even feel that their presence isn't required at all.

Many different sorts of things can become the object of a fetish, including shoes, feet, rubber, leather, silk, and women's underwear. Some people become dependent on sex-talk and need to hear a certain phrase repeated over and over while they're making love.

No one fully understands what causes a fetish but one theory is that it starts way back in childhood. Psychoanalysts think that the fetish object in some way represents love that the child didn't receive from its mother. They say that the object becomes sexualized and just as a small child has a teddy bear or a security blanket to hold on to when mom isn't there, the fetishist clings to the sex object for comfort. Another theory is that the fetish is a way of

regulating intimacy. If the fetishist lost someone close to them in the past, they may have developed a fear of future loss. This could be a way of coping with that fear, they sexualize an object and feel safer making love to it, rather than making love to the person behind it.

The subject of fetishes is quite fascinating and undoubtedly will continue to baffle analysts for many years. Meanwhile, a growing number of fetish enthusiasts are setting up clubs, magazines, and internet websites to provide more fodder for their various fantasies.

Flights of fantasy

Erotic fantasies seem to be a universal part of the human sexual experience. They've been around for aeons and young or old, rich or poor, male or female, we seem to fantasize about many of the same sorts of things, including sex with a stranger, and same-sex fantasies.

Understanding fantasies

A rich fantasy life can have many benefits for a sexual relationship. It can add novelty to a sex life that's beginning to lose its sparkle, it can provide an arena in which to practice alone before trying with a partner, and it can be very helpful for blocking out anxious thoughts. Some of us are aware of the source of our fantasies. These may relate to something once seen on TV, in a movie, magazine, or book. Other fantasies seem to come out of nowhere. How we feel about our sexual fantasies will depend largely on our sexual attitudes, and also our sexual tastes. Many people keep their fantasies private, fearing that if someone knew what turned them on, they would be considered weird or perverted.

Our sexual fantasies often express something that's deep within our unconscious mind and many of them seem to share a theme. Here are just a few of the most frequent ones:

Sex with a stranger

Sex with a stranger promises something new, exciting, and perfect. Without a doubt, the fantasized stranger will have a perfect body, perfect voice, and perfect sexual technique. And they'll be someone who sees you as being perfect in every way too. Fantasizing about sex with a stranger offers the opportunity to experience the perfect sexual encounter with no strings attached. Since you don't know them and will never see them again, you can enjoy sex for the sake of it, with no pretence and no price to pay.

Sex with more than one person

Many of us will have the occasional doubt as to whether or not we're able to sexually satisfy our partner. In fantasies about sex with more

than one person, these doubts are well and truly alleviated. Imagining having sex with more than one person means being attractive enough, horny enough, and fit enough to satisfy multiple appetites. This fantasy seems to be more common amongst men.

Same-sex fantasies

Fantasizing about having sex with someone of your own sex does not necessarily make you gay. Many heterosexual men and women have gay fantasies. Each of us will to a greater or lesser degree be attracted to people of our own gender at some stage in our lives. None of us is either gay or straight, we're somewhere in between. Same-sex fantasies are the unconscious mind's way of experimenting with the other side of ourselves. A few may want to try out their fantasies in real life, but most will be happy to enjoy their fantasies as a deeper expression of their sexual selves.

Watching and being watched

Sex is a private affair, particularly in our Western world. We expect people to keep their curtains closed and their bedroom doors firmly shut. It is precisely this secrecy and privacy that fuels the watching fantasies. Many of us get excited by doing something that we know

we're not really meant to do, so allowing ourselves to be seen whilst having sex, or watching on someone else can heighten the experience. Fantasizing about seeing other people having sex can be a way of learning. It can also allow us to be one step further removed from a sexual activity that we're not yet comfortable with.

Sex with an animal

This is perhaps one of the most troubling fantasies and one that is more prevalent amongst women, though statistics suggest that actual sex with animals is more common among men. Anyway, there seem to be two basic rationales for this fantasy. The first is that many people do become very attached to their pets. People form strong emotional bonds to their animals so perhaps it shouldn't be surprising that some people occasionally sexualize the relationship. The other thought is that sex with an animal has no ties or repercussions at all. Therefore it can be enjoyed as a purely sexual act with no emotional price to pay. This is one of the fantasies that is least likely to be acted out. Aside from the hygiene issues, most people who fantasize about sex with animals would consider it abusive to put their fantasy into practice.

Sharing sexual fantasies

Sharing a sexual fantasy involves a great degree of trust, particularly because once the fantasy is told, it cannot be untold. If you and your partner share similar fantasies then it's likely that sharing them will be a rewarding and enriching experience. Both of you are likely to feel more comfortable with your fantasy life and consequently you may expand your repertoire to include even more.

On the other hand, there are individuals who have shared a fantasy with their partner, only to be met with an embarrassed silence, shock, or even disgust. Fantasies are extremely personal and there are risks involved in disclosing them, especially to someone you care for. Sharing fantasies can be liberating, but only if they're accepted. If you think you'd like to share your fantasies, talk to your partner first about the general theme, then approach with extreme caution.

Acting out fantasies

Should you or should you not act out a fantasy? Of course, there is no right or wrong answer to this. As we've already explored, there are many fantasies that a person would never want to experience in real life. There are also those that they might not have the opportunity to do in real life. Those opportunities might not arise because of our inhibitions or our partner's inhibitions. Or we might not be able to act them out because either our partner or ourselves aren't physically capable.

If you would like to act out a fantasy, then obviously your partner needs to be interested in the idea as well. You should also consider how you will feel if the fantasy doesn't live up to your expectations. The reason fantasies are so sexually arousing is because

they are always perfect. Unfortunately, reality rarely is. Some people regret trying to act out their fantasies because it spoils them. The dream was not as good as they hoped and now the fantasy has lost its sparkle.

Whatever you choose to do with your fantasies, remember that ultimately, great sex is also about intimacy. There is only one good reason for sharing or acting out your fantasies and that is to enrich your relationship.

How will you feel if the reality doesn't live up to the fantasy?

TOP MALE FANTASIES

- Having sex with an existing partner.
- Giving and receiving oral sex.
- Sex with more than one person.
- Being dominant.
- Being passive and submissive.
- Reliving a previous experience.
- Watching others make love.
- New sexual positions.

TOP FEMALE FANTASIES

- Having sex with an existing partner.
- Reliving a previous experience.
- New sexual positions.
- Giving and receiving oral sex.
- Romantic or exotic locations.
- Being forced into sex.
- Being found irresistible.
- Sex with a new partner.
- Doing something forbidden.

The sacred stuff

A growing number of people are discovering the power and the ecstasy of sacred sex. Also known as High or Tantric Sex, followers of the tradition are promised erotic bliss, raised states of consciousness, and deeper intimacy with loved ones. This chapter introduces you to the basic principles and practices of this mystical art.

Sacred sex

The practice of sacred sex started in India in 5000 BCE through the cult of the Hindu god Shiva and his consort, the goddess Shakti. Hindus believe that when these ancient gods united sexually and spiritually, the universe was created. Thus, lovemaking not only generates the energy to create new life, but *all life*.

The origins of sacred sex

One of the ancient Eastern sciences of spiritual enlighten-ment was tantra. Unlike most other mystical paths, tantra includes sexuality as a doorway to ecstasy and enlightenment. Originally, it was practiced by Tibetan, Chinese, and Indian Buddhists as a sacred act, as their way of uniting the spirit with the flesh to attain enlightenment.

The word "tantra" means "weaving," unifying the many and often contradictory aspects of the self into one harmonious whole. It can also means "expansion," in the sense that once our energies are understood and woven together, we can grow into ultimate ecstasy.

The philosophy

Tantric philosophy, as in many other Eastern sciences, is based on the belief that our body has energy running through it in similarly to the way that blood runs through our veins. This energy connects the body's seven energy centers, or "chakras." It is believed that we can open up our chakras and move energy through these channels to create a sensation of wholeness.

Sacred sex is meditative and gentle, transforming the energy of sexual arousal into an experience of pure ecstasy. Rather than sex which is energetic and vigorous building up to a final orgasmic explosive release, the tantric couple glide through sexual ecstasy, experiencing orgasm throughout

the body and brain. Sacred sex unites body, mind, and spirit, as well as two people.

There is no goal in tantric sex, only the present moment of perfect and harmonious union. Since the focus is on wholeness, tantra embraces everyone and every type of sexual practice. There is no sense of right or wrong. Everything is acceptable, as long as it can be understood and integrated. It doesn't matter who you have sex with, what matters is that each person respects each other's sacred potential and is open to enter full communion within their own body and with each other. Tantra teaches you to revere your sexual partner and to transform the act of sex into a sacrament of love.

Sacred sex is meditative and gentle

Sacred sex is a mystical subject that is almost impossible to define. Its very essence is about getting in touch with your inner self and no one has yet come up with a definitive definition to explain that process.

To gain fuller understanding of this mystical practice, it may be advisable to invest in one of the many books dedicated to the subject. I recommend *The New Art of Sexual Ecstasy* by Margo Anand that takes you step-by-step through a wide range of methods to enhance pleasure and deepen intimacy.

The practices

The basic tenet is that ecstasy is within all of us. Sacred sex teaches you to discover your own inner energy, mobilize it, and express it, harnessing and containing sexual energy rather than releasing it. The essence is to be able to get fully in touch with your powerful sexual energy, learn to channel it through the seven chakras, and all the while remaining physically relaxed.

The tension you are used to feeling as you build toward orgasm has to be relaxed into and thereby spread around the rest of the body. So rather than localized genital sensations, the experience of arousal is felt throughout. At orgasm, rather than just a genital release, the whole body ripples with wavelike pulses. This is

known as the full-body orgasm, said to be equal to an altered state of consciousness. When two of you experience this together, the energy between your bodies melts and merges and you can enjoy complete sexual communion.

Each practice follows the same formula, that of seeking a deep sense of satisfaction or positive energy, and staying with it, deepening it, becoming one with it, maintaining focus, and entering into an even deeper sense of awareness. Each time you do this, you expand and build your potential for ecstasy. Over time, with much patience and focus, you will familiariarize yourself with the sensations and more proficient at channeling your energy until it becomes second nature.

In its most authentic form, tantra prohibits male ejaculation because it is believed to waste sexual energy. However, women are encouraged to learn how to ejaculate

In tantra the vagina is called the *yoni*, meaning "sacred space" and the penis is known as the *lingam* meaning "wand of light." The term most commonly used for sexual energy is *kundalini* which also means "life force."

Sacred self

The first principle of sacred sex is that you must find within yourself the potential for sexual ecstasy without feelings of guilt or shame. Sacred sex is dependent upon finding your own internal capacity for high levels of sexual pleasure. Once you've discovered this, then you're ready to share it with a partner.

Getting ready for sacred sex

Initial practices focus on finding your "inner lover" through relaxation and visualization. Your inner lover is the piece of yourself that totally accepts you as you are, the part of you that loves you and supports you and has always been there for you and always will. One exercise for achieving this is to allow yourself to become fully relaxed and remember a time when you felt truly loved. That might be as a child in your mother's arms or with a lover. Spending time relaxing into those feelings again can help us remember that we are lovable and cared for. Regularly performing this exercise can help build self-esteem.

Tantra also requires positive body confidence. This means more than just learning to love the way our body looks, but also to

learn to trust our body's innate wisdom. The body and mind should be fully integrated. Rather than just thinking about what is good, one must learn to sense it with the body. The body is the

vehicle for our spirit and in tantra it is essential that each part of the body is honored. Many tantric teachers recommend the "ceremony of recognition" to help to achieve this.

THE CEREMONY OF RECOGNITION

This exercise helps build acceptance and confidence in each part of the body and thereby build sexual potential.

Start by making sure you're in a sensual, warm, and safe environment where you won't be interrupted. Then, either sitting or standing in front of a full-length mirror, apply body lotion or perfume to each part of your body. Do this with love and care and as you touch each part of yourself, repeat the affirmations below:

My feet are the vehicle of my spirit and I honor them
My legs are the vehicle of my spirit and I honor them
My hands are the vehicle of my spirit and I honor them
My arms are the vehicle of my spirit and I honor them
My pelvis is the vehicle of my spirit and I honor it
My genitals are the vehicle of my spirit and I honor them
My belly is the vehicle of my spirit and I honor it
My heart is the vehicle of my spirit and I honor it
My chest is the vehicle of my spirit and I honor it
My throat is the vehicle of my spirit and I honor it
My mouth are the vehicle of my spirit and I honor it
My eyes are the vehicle of my spirit and I honor them
The crown of my head is the vehicle of my spirit and I honor it

When you have completed this, take some time to relax, and end by placing your hands on your heart and saying: "My body is the temple of my spirit and I honor it."

The next step in discovering your sacred self is to get in touch with and expand your sexual energy. First you need to recognize and focus on the sexual energy within the sexual center, or sex chakra. Once this energy is located, it can be channeled up through the seven chakras to the crown chakra. The crown chakra is the centre of higher creativity where the realms of peace, wonderment, and ecstasy can be experienced. Once you get used to transforming this sexual energy and allowing it to travel throughout your body, you will be ready for a much fuller experience of arousal and orgasm. One method for recognizing and building sexual energy is the pelvic rock exercise. Once you've mastered this, you can channel the energy through the chakras by using sexual breathing techniques.

The pelvic rock

This exercise will help to increase pelvic flexibility and energy.

Stand with your feet flat on the floor, parallel and shoulder-width apart. Now bend your knees slightly as if you were skiing. Keep your back straight and shoulders and arms relaxed. Now begin by gently rocking your pelvis. Be sure that your back is not moving, just your pelvis. Practice curling your pelvis forward in a thrusting motion, just as you might make in intercourse. Hold this position for a moment and then allow your pelvis to curl backward. This is a more gentle movement and will feel as though you're just letting your pelvis move back to its natural position. Continue this rocking motion for a few minutes, being sure that the rest of your body remains relaxed.

Now coordinate breathing with rocking. Breathe in deeply as you rock backward and exhale energetically as you thrust forward. Some people find it helpful to say "ha!" as they breathe out. Continue to practice this exercise until your speed quickens and you feel your comfort and confidence increasing.

Sexual breathing

Once you've mastered the pelvic rock and have increased your energy, it's time to practice expanding the energy up through the seven chakras.

Start by making yourself comfortable and relaxed. Lie down and let your hands gently rest on, and cup, your genitals. Now breathe gently in through puckered lips, hearing the sound as you inhale, then relax your lips and gently exhale. Continue for a few moments, getting into your body's natural rhythm. When you're ready, contract and hold your PC muscles (see page 22) as you breathe in, and relax them as you breathe out.

Now. as you inhale, and contract your PC muscles, visualize the entering though your genitals and flowing all the way up through your body to the crown of your head. As you exhale and relax your PC muscles, visualize the air flowing back down your body and out through your genitals.

You can further enhance this exercise by allowing one hand to travel up the body following the line of your breath while the other stays on your genitals. Be sure to remain as focused as possible and fully aware of the energy traveling up and down, up and down.

Sacred masturbation

As with every other form of sacred or tantric sex, the aim of masturbation is to move beyond the focus on the genitals to a full-body experience. Self-pleasuring is expanded so that you reach the pinnacle of pleasure. Rather than concentrating on the orgasm, hold the tension, relax into the sensations, and send the energy through the chakras. Each time the waves of pleasure rise they are pushed to the body extremes until the final release of orgasm is experienced in the heart, mind, soul, and genitals.

Start to masturbate the tantric way, slowly and sensually. Begin by creating your environment. Many people enjoy listening to rhythmical and arousing music. A wide range of music is now available to complement sacred sexual experiences. You might also want to light candles, spray scent, or burn aromatherapy oil.

The next step is to ensure you are using your mind. Sacred masturbation involves becoming your own lover and cherishing your own body. This can be enhanced by visualization, such as thinking back to a sexual encounter with a loved one or imagining an erotic scene.

With your mind and senses in harmony, you can begin to enjoy touch. Starting by stroking your body all over, allowing yourself time to get fully in touch with the sensual delights of the skin. Then slowly and gradually begin to caress your genitals in a way that you find arousing. But remember, your goal is not reach orgasm as quickly as possible, but to move

your sexual arousal throughout your body.

Moving sexual arousal

When you begin to feel arousal building in your genitals, you need to consciously expand it to the other chakras.

As you stimulate yourself with one hand, allow the other hand to caress your abdominal area. Focus on your breathing and visualize your arousal spreading into your lower abdomen. Feel the warmth in those areas and expand it by using the sexual breathing technique. Breathe the energy in through your genitals and allow the pleasurable sensations to fill your entire abdomen. When you feel you are at the point of orgasm, stop stimulation and breathe in deeply. Hold the arousal energy in and visualize it

spreading out into your abdomen. Hold this point for as long as you comfortably can, then relax and exhale.

To move the energy further up the chakras, begin stimulation again in a slow and steady fashion. Allow the feelings to build again and just before the point of orgasm, take a sharp, deep intake of breath, contract your PC muscles, and visualize the arousal moving even further up toward your heart center. You may find that stroking your body from your hands to your heart will help you to visualize the movement of the energy.

Continue in this way three times more, then allow yourself to orgasm. Once you have mastered moving the energy up to the heart center, you can gradually begin to practice drawing the energy up to the other chakras.

Sacred partners

The principles of sexual ecstasy with a partner assume that you have already found that potential within yourself. Having achieved this, you can share what you've learned with your partner and prepare for a higher union of souls that starts by honoring your partner.

Sacred space is where you and your partner share a heart-to-heart connection

This higher union starts with honoring your partner, accepting their uniqueness, and recognizing them as a divine lover. A common ritual for lovers to greet each other and show their commitment to sacred sex is the Heart Salutation. It is inspired by the traditional *namaste* greeting used in the East, signifying "I honor the God within you."

Greeting each other in this way prepares you for entering into a sacred space, somewhere where you and your partner share a heart-to-heart connection, somewhere full of love, trust, and respect. It is also somewhere in which any fears of sexual intimacy have been fully explored and overcome through honest communication and mutual acceptance.

Connecting energy

Once you are in touch with each other's sexual potential, you can begin to connect your energies. Being able to tune into each other's energy helps to share and connect at a much deeper level than you may ever have experienced before. This involves stilling the mind and giving each other 100% of your attention. As well as helping you both unwind from a busy day at work and reconnecting as lovers, it can be a beautiful way of beginning a session of sacred sex.

HEART SALUTATION

You need to allow at least 10 minutes for this exercise when you will not be disturbed. Though the exercise may seem very simple, it can be very powerful.

Start by sitting facing your partner. Gaze gently into each other's eyes for a few moments and then bring the palms of your cupped hands together in front of you, resting your thumbs against your chest.

Now close your eyes and as you exhale, both of you should gently bend forward from the waist, keeping your backs straight. Bend forward at a 45degree angle until your foreheads lightly touch. Hold this connection for a few minutes, focusing on the openness and respect that this gesture conveys.

When you're both ready, sit up straight, open your eyes, look into your partner's eyes, and say "(Name) I honor the god/goddess within you."

GAZING

Begin with a heart salutation, then sit facing your partner. Breathe deeply and lightly hold hands. Begin by closing your eyes for a few moments and allow yourself to become fully conscious of the current moment. When you are ready, open your eyes and gaze deeply into your partner's left eye. The left eye is considered to be the "receptive eye" that allows the energy of the other person in. Direct your complete attention to your gaze and allow your breathing to become synchronized. Start by performing this exercise for just five minutes at a time and gradually lengthen the time when you are both ready.

Tantric lovers are encouraged to masturbate while holding the other's gaze

Masturbating together

Breaking through inhibition is essential to achieving sacred sex, since inhibitions restrict and stifle sexual energy. A good way is to learn to masturbate in each other's presence.

Tantric lovers are encouraged to masturbate while holding the other's gaze in full eye contact. This experience can empower them both. Each is able to take responsibility for their own sexual release and show how they like to be touched. They can also feel free from the pressure of thinking they are the sole source of their partner's pleasure.

When stimulating each other, lovers are also encouraged to maintain eye contact and communicate as they build their partner's sexual energy and expand it through the chakras. The tantric couple learn to flow in tune with each other's energy, to ride ever higher levels of arousal before holding their partner as they relax into the sensations, and build and ride again.

Sacred sex and the *Kama Sutra*

The *Kama Sutra* has become synonymous with sacred sex and has formed the underpinning of other forms such as tantra. The *Kama Sutra*—meaning "guide of the Hindu God of Love"—is the earliest surviving example of a love-manual. Compiled by the Indian sage Vatsyayana sometime between the second and fourth centuries, this work was based on earlier Kama Shastras, or "Rules of Love," going back to at least the seventh century BCE. It is a compendium of the social norms and love customs of Northern India at around that time.

The *Kama Sutra* is divided into seven parts: general remarks, amorous advances, acquiring a wife, duties and privileges of a wife, relations with other men's wives, and a section about courtesans and occult means. The final part includes formulations for medicines, with the emphasis on aphrodisiacs.

In the 16th century, Indian love sage Kalyana Malla wrote the *Ananga Ranga*. This was similar to the *Kama Sutra* but the focus was on keeping sex exciting and interesting for monogamous couples. There is much emphasis on breaking patterns of laziness and familiarity and encouraging long-term lovers to use their minds and imaginations to achieve higher levels of eroticism. Unlike the *Kama Sutra*, that accepted that a man will have many lovers, the *Ananga Ranga* teaches lovers to experience their partner as if they were 32 different lovers.

Sacred positions

Tantra is based on the basic lovemaking positions from the *Kama Sutra*. The five basic lovemaking positions are:

• The man on his back with the woman on top.

• The woman on her back with the man on top.

• The woman and man on their sides, facing each other.

• The rear-entry position with the man in back of the woman.

• The woman and man both seated, usually facing each other.

The Yab Yum position is considered one of the most powerfully intimate positions in tantra. Yab Yum means "mother-and-father union" and provides maximum physical contact and the opportunity to align the chakras of the body so that sexual energy can be shared.

This is a seated position. The woman should sit on her partner's lap facing him with her legs wrapped tightly around his waist. Both partners should have their arms wrapped around each other. Without thrusting, the couple can

focus on their individual sexual energy and expand it through the seven chakras in synchronization as they melt into mutual sexual ecstasy.

There is no doubt that many people have experienced profound intimacy and sexual ecstasy through the practice of sacred sex. However, even the tantric masters

confess that they can't remain on those dizzy heights forever and there are times when sex is still less than perfect. What sacred sex offers is basic principles for good sexual experience as an alternative to goal-orientated genital sex. It also provides for positive self-esteem, sexual variety, and open and honest communication between partners.

A
Lifetime
of
sex

Sex changes dramatically during our lifetimes, and accepting this fact can help you to enjoy it all the more. This chapter gives advice on keeping sex exciting in long-term relationships, as well as exploring the impact of parenting and aging on a couple's sex life.

Keeping sex sexy

Sex in a long-term relationship does not have to become boring. The couples who expect sex to become boring will almost certainly find that it will, while those that work together to keep sex sexy ensure that it won't. Whether sex is boring or not, is all about attitude and commitment.

Many couples remember with great fondness the heady days of passion when they first got together. When you fall in love, sex is urgent and exciting. It's a new experience fueled with adrenalin and passion. You're desperate to learn more about each other, especially about each other's bodies. Sex is often used as a way of showing how much you love each other but as your confidence in the relationship grows, you will find other ways in which to express love and affection.

When you move in together, sex may become less of a priority. This is partly because of all the other things that need to be done to run a home together, but also because now you can have sex whenever you want to. Sex becomes more of a choice, one of the many things that you enjoy doing together, rather than the only thing.

As your relationship matures, sex matures as well, but like a fine wine, it should become richer and fruitier. As you get to know each other better, a deeper trust develops. You're less likely to feel inhibited and you can look forward to a new stage of sexual experimentation. Without the initial insecurities, you can take the time to learn to become great lovers together.

Committed to sex and sensuality

Couples who make a commitment to keep their sex life exciting and fulfilling accept that sex changes. They accept that the mere sight of their partner may not always send them into a lustful frenzy and they know that sex can become predictable if they always do the same things. And because they know this, they agree that as their relationship continues to mature, they will

make more effort not less.

They commit to being romantic and seductive with each other, no matter how well they know each other. They make an effort to always look their best and make time to enjoy each other's company. They make touch and affectionate words important parts of their daily routine.

They also agree not to fall for the myth that great sex has to be spontaneous. This means that, regardless of how busy their diaries are, they make time to be sensual and sexual. They certainly don't fall for the myth that lust equals love. They know that they must take responsibility for their own sexual desires and also find new ways to turn each other on.

Couples who still enjoy a great sex life after 10, 20, or even 50 years together, aren't lucky they're committed. They have recognized the boredom traps and opted out of them swiftly.

Boredom traps

There are certain signs that sex is becoming boring. You can either choose to ignore these signs, or do something about it. It's not always easy, especially if your partner seems to be happy with things the way they are. But ultimately, great sex is about both of you being happy. If you become aware of slipping into any of the following boredom traps, then talk to your partner and address the issue before it becomes a problem.

PUSHING THE BOUNDARIES

Many couples hanker after being more adventurous but are nervous about raising the subject. One way to do this is to agree to each write down three things on separate pieces of paper. Share your ideas and then fold the papers and put them in a hat or the bedside drawer. Next time you're making love, pick something new out of the hat to try.

Or perhaps something a little more seductive but equally up front: "I want you now." Try it, they might like it.

Silent and frenzied

Start with a hug and kiss, but turn up the tempo quickly so your partner is left in no doubt as to what you want. To make this even more of a surprise, do it while they're in the middle of something else, maybe doing the dishes or washing the car.

Daring and erotic

This takes guts, since obviously you can't guarantee the response, but what the heck? Either naked or dressed up in something sexy, be ready to meet and greet your unsuspecting partner with an offer you hope they can't refuse.

An easy way to inject extra energy into your sex life is to change the way you initiate sex

The same come-on

Do you or your partner always use the same come-on line? Many couples slip into the same boring, predictable initiation routines. If she says: "I fancy an early night," or he says: "You look cute tonight," that means sex is on the cards. It may be the same sly smile or wink, or the wandering hand under the bedclothes. Whatever it is, do you think: "Oh great!" or: "Here we go again"? If it's the latter, then you're slipping into the boredom trap.

A quick and easy way to inject extra energy into your sex life is to change the way you initiate. You have a number of options.

Romantic

The candlelit dinner, a massage, a foot rub, or anything tender and caring that says, "I love you."

Bold and brazen

"How about it?" may seem rather abrupt, but said with a wink and a hug it might be warmly received.

The same time

Perhaps you don't really initiate sex at all anymore and it has turned into a routine, an every Friday night affair. You may never have intentionally set this up, it's never been put into words, but for some reason, it's always on the same day at the same time. Routine is a real passion-killer.

Sex doesn't have to be at bedtime. Now, everybody knows that, but it is surprising how many couples seem to struggle to do it at any other time. The best way to beat the habit is to reintroduce the quickie. A quickie before work, while the kids are still in bed, before friends come round, or you go shopping. Or all four. You probably wouldn't want your entire sex life to be made up of quickies, but the occasional one can stop sex becoming predictable.

The same place

We also know that sex doesn't always have to happen in bed. But unfortunately it becomes another

one of those routines that many couples slip into. Even when you've mastered a range of come-ons and regularly enjoy a quickie, you still head up to the bedroom.

A great way to spice up your sex life is to change the scenery. It'll probably also make you more adventurous with sexual positions. Remember the shower, the tub, the sofa, in front of the fire, up against a door, over the kitchen table, on a chair. Or go al fresco, either in your own back yard, or go for a walk, take the travel rug, and see where your passion takes you.

The same technique

So now you're having sex on Saturday morning in the shower after a surprise come-on—so what next? If you want to stop orgasms becoming mundane, then you need to keep changing and adapting your technique. Just because your partner enjoyed a certain thing five or 10 years ago,

it doesn't mean they still do. When was the last time you gave each other a sensual massage and checked out the erogenous zones? When was the last time you tried a new sexual position or varied your oral or manual technique? And what about the adventurous stuff? Sex toys and games, dressing up, an erotic movie?

It really doesn't matter what you do as long as you're not offending your partner and are adding variety and interest. Sometimes you'll have to stretch beyond your comfort zones. You might occasionally agree to do something new that you're not fully sure about. But this is the great advantage of a long-term relationship, the extra trust and security means you don't have to fear rejection or embarrassment if it doesn't work out. You're both in this together and you're both committed to keeping sex as sexy as possible.

10 QUICK & EASY WAYS TO KEEP SEX SEXY

1. Change the scenery—bathroom, living room, al fresco.
2. Watch an erotic movie together to get you in the mood.
3. Change position—sitting, standing, over a table.
4. Introduce a new sex toy.
5. Change the come-on—romantic, brazen or erotic.
6. Have a quickie at any or every time of day.
7. Play some sex games: Doctors and nurses, slave & master, etc.
8. Learn a new oral technique.
9. Have a play fight.
10. Share a fantasy.

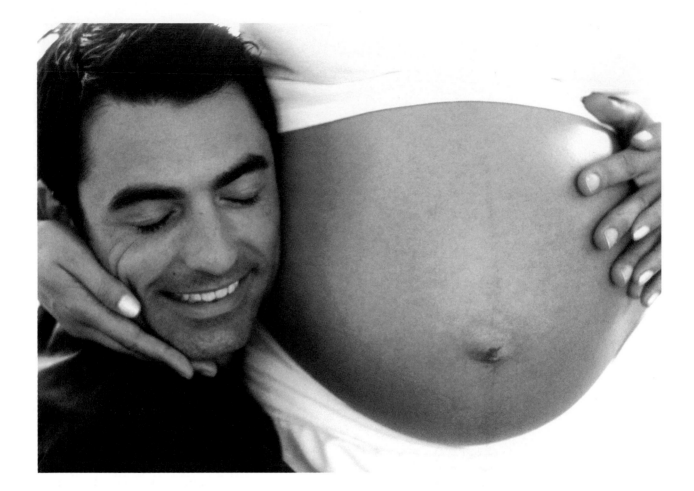

Sex and parenting

Whether you're trying to make babies, just had one, or waiting for one to leave home, your sex life will not be the same. Parenting takes an emotional and physical toll on any couple. It is important to be aware that your relationship will move into a whole new era and so will your sex life.

Trying for a baby

When you're trying for a baby, sex takes on a whole new meaning. Not only are you sharing intimate time together and enjoying physical pleasure, but you're also creating a new life. For years, this may have been something you've strenuously avoided, but now it's your reason for being.

For most couples, this is an excellent excuse for having a lot more sex. The more sex you have, the quicker you're likely to conceive. Here are some other tips for hitting the jackpot:

Give up smoking

This is important for both of you. Smoking affects male fertility and can increase the chances of miscarriage if you conceive.

Reduce alcohol intake

Alcohol affects the quality of sperm, so you should cut back.

Eat a healthy diet

Make sure you're getting plenty of fresh fruit and vegetables, and protein-rich foods. Women are recommended to take a folic acid supplement.

Minimize stress

Stress causes hormonal changes in the body that can make it harder to conceive.

Keep cool

Men should bear in mind that sperm has to be below body temperature. Avoid hot baths and wear boxer shorts to improve air flow!

Have sex at the right time

Make sure you're having loads of sex around ovulation time. This will be around 14 days after the start of a period. Some women's cycles are less regular than others, in which case you might find an ovulation testing kit useful. Others rely on the mucus check. In the first and last weeks of the cycle, your vaginal mucus will be thick and sticky, but around ovulation time it is thin and watery—the right consistency to let the sperm into the cervix.

It can take time to conceive, so it's important that you keep your sex life fun. An average couple in their twenties take five months to conceive, in their early thirties, they take an average of nine months. Ten percent of couples take over a year.

Don't fall into the trap of making sex a chore that must be performed only around ovulation. It's true that male sperm counts are slightly lower if they have frequent sex, but since each ejaculation contains literally millions of sperm, you really won't miss a few.

Sex and infertility

If you've been trying for a baby for more than 12 months, it may be time to visit the doctor.

This can be a very difficult time for couples. Medical interventions and procedures can make sex appear clinical. Fear of being told that either or both of you can't conceive could leave you wondering whether sex might even be a futile activity.

During this time, you may find that sex becomes a chore, with the goal being conception. Having fun, being playful, and sharing physical intimacy take second place. Try to remember that, as well as being the way of creating new life, sex has the power to comfort, support, and relax. You can enjoy making love as a way of consoling and encouraging each other during this difficult time.

SEXUAL POSITIONS THAT ARE BELIEVED TO IMPROVE CHANCES OF CONCEPTION

There are no definitive studies to support this, but many experts believe the old-fashioned missionary position is the best. They also suggest that putting a pillow under the woman's rear end and staying in that position for 30 minutes after ejaculation will make it easier for the sperm to swim downhill toward the cervix. Woman on top, standing, and sitting positions are discouraged because they defy gravity. If the woman has an orgasm after the man, this will further help conception, as the contractions help to draw the sperm into the cervix.

Sex during pregnancy

How couples feel about sex during pregnancy varies enormously. For some, it's a huge relief not to be trying for a baby any more. The deed is done, the job was a success, and now sex can go back to being purely recreational. For other couples, it can feel slightly strange. Now there aren't just two of you making love—there's someone else there too.

Sex will feel different during the stages of pregnancy. In the first three months before there's an obvious bump, sex might feel pretty much the same as it always did. Unfortunately, many women are plagued with nausea and tiredness in early pregnancy, which can have a very detrimental effect on libido. For a few couples the first three months are also an anxious time, as miscarriage is most likely then.

In the second three months, baby is going to be making much more of an appearance. This is a time when some women need extra reassurance about how they look. Some women think they've never looked better, while others become self-conscious of their growing breasts and belly. It's also during these months that many women experience genital swelling. As extra blood is pumped to the pelvic region, many pregnant women feel more sexually aroused than ever before, and their orgasms can feel particularly intense.

In the final three months, the baby is heading for full size and couples need to become more creative with sexual positions. Many couples find that rear positions are most comfortable and, for some, the only ones that are feasible. Spoons is another position that many couples enjoy.

During the second trimester, many women feel more sexually aroused

Many new parents don't feel like having sex after the birth of a new baby. Take some time during pregnancy to sit down and discuss how you will handle this as a couple

Some women and men find their desire for sex waning more and more as they head for the nine-month mark. This is due to a growing preoccupation with the impending delivery and excitement of becoming a parent.

Sex after childbirth

The first few weeks after a baby is born are often the most exhausting weeks in a couple's life. Whether you're breast-feeding or bottle-feeding, it's extremely unlikely that your newborn is going to sleep through the night. For many couples, the sheer newness of the situation is tiring. There are so many extra things to consider. On top of earning a living and maintaining a home, there are diapers, feeds, nursery rhymes, and hundreds of relatives to visit. As you are adjusting to the new role of parenting, sex can be one of the last things on your mind.

In addition, 80% of new moms report reduced sexual desire in the first few months. This is due to exhaustion and to hormonal changes. Knowing that the body needs to get back to full strength again and energy needs to be focused on the new baby, Mother Nature temporarily depletes the sex hormones to ensure that brothers and sisters don't arrive too soon.

During this time it's essential that couples keep talking to each other. Moms and dads can feel guilty about not wanting sex. Being able to share how you feel together and supporting each other in the early months will help you to maintain intimacy and your identity as a couple.

Whether you're ready to have sex again or not and no matter how infrequent it may be over the coming months, remember that you are still lovers as well as parents.

WHEN YOU DON'T WANT SEX

Remember, you can still be lovers even if you're not having sex. Take time to be sensual together, share a bath or a shower, have a massage, take time to kiss and hug. Keeping the romance alive will help you to slip naturally back into your sex life when the time is right for you both.

When the kids are small

If you thought it was tough finding time for sex when you had a baby, wait until you've got a couple of toddlers zooming around the house! The great advantage of this time is that it forces you to get creative about your lovemaking. If you've begun to slip into any routines, the kids will probably force you out of them.

You'll need to learn to be flexible. Long, lustful sessions will probably need to be pre-arranged to ensure you don't get disturbed, but with a little forethought, there are plenty of opportunities for quickies. Here are just a few ideas:

Bedtime

If at all possible, make sure the kids are in bed at the same time. But don't wait until it's your bedtime to make love or you'll probably both be too exhausted. Have sex, then have dinner, and relax.

Nap times

If you manage for your children to nap at the same time, DO NOT take this opportunity to do the ironing—unless of course, you still have time when you've finished having sex!

Videos/Kids' TV

Little kids will sit bug-eyed watching TV for quite long periods of time. As long as you know they're safe, this, is the perfect opportunity to rush upstairs.

Babysitters

If you're going out for an evening, ask the babysitter to come an hour early, so you can both get ready without any distractions. The babysitter will welcome the extra money and the two of you can enjoy a passionate encounter in the bathroom as part of your evening preparations.

Grandma

Or any other responsible adult who might be able to have the children for a whole day, afternoon, evening, or night at their house. Make the most of knowing you won't be interrupted and use the time for a long, slow, sensual lovemaking session, just like you used to have.

When the kids are old enough to know what you're really doing

Small children are fairly easy to fob off, if indeed they even notice you've left the room. Older children are quite a different matter. A young child probably won't question mommy and daddy cuddling under the comforter or being told, "Not now we're talking." But older children will either hang around inquisitively, or worse, they'll know exactly what you're doing.

For many parents, this is an anxious time. You want to keep your sex life alive and hopefully you don't believe you're too old to have a good time, even if that's what your kids think. But you have to walk a thin line between honesty and openness and your privacy. Older children and teenagers will feel embarrassed if they know you're having sex, so a certain amount of subtlety may be necessary to respect their sensitivity. But if you're always going to wait until there's absolutely no chance of them suspecting what you're up to, then your sex life might become very sparse indeed.

Again, this is a time when planning and creativity is required. Consider the following:

An early night

It is surprising how soon the kids stay up as late as you do, or even later. This is when "We're having an early night" needs to become a regular occurrence.

Videos/DVDs/TV

With a TV and video/DVD player in your bedroom you can go upstairs to watch one of your own while the kids are absorbed with their own programs. This is a great opportunity to share an erotic movie (keep the remote handy in case there's a knock at the door), and you'll obviously want an early night when it's finished.

Extra-curricular activities

If at all possible, coordinate when children are out. There are many out-of-school activities and it shouldn't take too much effort to either send

them to the same event or class. This allows you both at least a couple of hours a week uninterrupted.

While they're out

Older children and teenagers are often out of the house in the early evenings and in the daytime at weekends. Don't use this time to cut the grass or go shopping, because it is the perfect opportunity for sex. If you're worried about them coming home earlier than expected, slip the latch on the front door.

Sleepovers

Again, coordination is the key. If one child is going to be out at a sleepover, encourage the other(s) to go too.

It doesn't matter how you make time for sex, it's just essential that you do. Not only are you keeping the intimacy alive in your relationship but you're also setting a good example for the kids. Seeing parents who are affectionate and sensual with each other encourages children to work toward a good physical relationship when they're older.

LOCK UP

If you're nervous about a young child walking in on you, put a lock on the bedroom door. If you do this when a child is very young they will accept it as regular, and learn to knock. If you can't fob them off with "not now we're talking about your birthday/Christmas presents," or if it's an emergency, you can still leap out of bed and open the door.

Sex and aging

It may seem like only yesterday that you were reading up on sex in pregnancy and now, suddenly the kids are leaving home. You may have spent many years wishing you had more time for each other, more time to make love, but when you do finally get it, it can be a shock.

Suddenly finding you have the house to yourselves and can do whatever you like when you like, can be a little daunting. Many couples have been so busy raising a family that their sex life has taken second place. Now, there's only the two of you. You can make love on the living-room rug in the middle of the day or over the kitchen table at breakfast time if you so wish.

This provides you both with an excellent opportunity to rediscover some of the sexual delights that you might have forgotten. You have more time, and probably more money too, to spend on pampering yourself and pampering each other.

This is also the time of life when bodies are changing and getting older. You realize that you're not as fit as you used to be. The sexual olympics you enjoyed in the early years are far more likely to do you an injury now, unless you've kept yourself in shape. However, the good news is, you've now got far more time to get yourself in shape.

Fit for sex

The healthier and fitter you are, the better your sex life will be. As we age, our bodies become less supple and more prone to injury. Now is an excellent time to take up those Yoga or Pilates classes that you were always planning on doing. Improving your muscle tone, cardiovascular system, and your flexibility will not only help you remain sexually active for many years to come, but you might discover you can enjoy sexual positions that would challenge a 20-year-old!

Regular exercise promotes stamina and energy. In fact, research has consistently shown that men and women who are fit and active enjoy more regular and

more fulfilling sex lives. Regular exercise keeps us looking good too, and if we feel confident about how we look, we're likely to feel more confident in bed.

So keeping fit will help to keep you sexual. But the reverse is also true. Couples who continue to have an active sex life are also likely to keep fit and age more slowly (or at least look as though they are). An active sex life produces a variety of chemicals that helps us to feel happy, enhances the immune system, increases lean body tissue, and thickens skin tissue. One survey concluded that improving the quality of your sex life can help make you look between four and seven years younger, reduce stress, and lead to greater contentment.

A really passionate sex session can burn off around 200 calories—the same as a 15-minute jog

REMEMBER WHEN?

If you've forgotten how sex was BC (before children), then try this exercise. Take a sheet of paper each and allow yourselves a good 30 minutes to brainstorm some of the best sex sessions you can remember. Think about vacation times, different rooms in the house, special occasions, risqué moments, etc. When you've each finished, share your lists and see what the memories spark off.

Physical changes

Sex in later life has many advantages. In many ways, men and women are more equally matched. Most men will have lost their earlier physical urgency for satisfaction and many women feel more confident and comfortable with their sexuality. You both know each other really well and hopefully you feel happy to talk to each other about the changing needs of your body.

Some physical changes will be due to the natural aging process while others might be the result of illness or a side effect of medication. Common illnesses such as diabetes, heart disease, and blood pressure problems directly affect sexual functioning, while other conditions such as arthritis have more of an indirect affect. But if you're both aware of those changes and ready and willing to accommodate them in your love making, you can continue to enjoy an active and fulfilling sex life well into your eighties.

Changes in women

The changes in women's sexuality are most obviously heralded by the menopause. For most women this starts at around age fifty and can last for between five and 15 years. The slow and gradual reduction of estrogen is responsible for the range of emotional and physical changes that women experience.

The most obvious physical symptoms are irregular periods that then stop altogether, There are also sweats and hot flashes, drier hair and skin, joint pain, and tiredness. Emotional changes include feeling moody and irritable, and having difficulty sleeping and concentrating.

For many women, menopause is a difficult time, though most don't experience severe problems.

Increasingly women are turning to Hormone Replacement Therapy (HRT) to manage any troublesome side effects.

Impact on sex

Lowered sexual desire

Lower levels of estrogen and testosterone can reduce sexual desire, though it is more likely to be a side effect of general menopausal symptoms. Making sure you take extra time to get in the mood and being sensual together should help you to overcome this problem.

Painful intercourse

The walls of the vagina become thinner and less lubrication is produced. It also takes longer to get aroused as you get older. So it's essential to take plenty of time to get fully aroused and you could also ask your doctor to prescribe an estrogen cream to ease lubrication problems.

Delayed orgasm

Some women find that it takes them longer to orgasm than it

52% of men and 36% of women are still sexually active in their seventies

used to and the sensation is not quite so strong. This is mostly due to the fact that it takes longer to get aroused in the first place. Remember, time is on your side so take as much of it as you need.

Many women say they enjoy sex more after the menopause than they did before. This could be because they have more confidence, their partners are more experienced, they no longer have to worry about contraception—or all three. Since a third of a woman's life is now likely to be post-menopausal, it's certainly worth taking the time to enjoy great sex.

Changes in men

The male menopause—or andropause—has only been taken seriously by the medical profession relatively recently. There are still conflicting views as to whether this is a physical or psychological condition in men, but certainly the midlife crisis is nothing new.

Many men experience tiredness and fatigue, increased irritability, reduced muscle mass, generalized aches and pains, sweating, and general moodiness. Since testosterone levels are known to reduce gradually over the life cycle, some physicians are now offering a testosterone patch to help men with andropause symptoms. Many men who have been treated in this way say that it has eased their symptoms though it's not clear whether or not this is just a placebo effect.

Impact on sex

Reduced desire

Many men say that their desire for sex is less frequent and less urgent than, say, in their twenties.

Slower to arouse

Once upon a time, the thought of sex would have caused an instant erection, but many older men will need direct penile stimulation in order to become aroused.

Less firm erections

The sensation of erection is likely to be less than it was, though it will still be quite firm enough for penetration.

Slower ejaculation

For many men, this side effect of aging is one they value. The urgency to ejaculate tends to reduce significantly, so a mature lover can last longer. Ejaculation may also feel less powerful than in earlier days.

Older men often make better, more confident lovers. With the urgency for orgasm reduced, most men are able to enjoy the intricacies of touching and pleasing their partner rather than worrying about their performance.

It's never too late for great sex

As I discovered when writing this book together, it's really difficult to find positive images of older couples enjoying sex, or even being naked. When the media portrays great sex it's always between a virile, athletic young

men and a slim, nubile young women. It's not surprising that many people assume that great sex is only for the young and beautiful.

But society's views are changing. The population of older adults is increasing and all those originators of free love in the '60s are hitting sixty themselves and challenging the stereotypes of the aging couple.

As we've seen, sex changes as you become older, but it doesn't have to become any less enjoyable. As long as there's no debilitating illness, there is no reason why couples can't thoroughly enjoy sex as long as they live—in fact, they're likely to live a darn site longer if they do!

"Most people give up sex for the same reasons they stop riding a bicycle: 1) They think it looks silly; 2) They have arthritis and can't get on; 3) They don't own a bicycle."
Dr. Alex Comfort, author of
The Joy of Sex

Sexual problems

Sexual difficulties affect all of us at some stage in our lives. Sometimes we know the cause to be illness, stress, a new baby, or perhaps just too much to drink. At other times, they may come out of the blue. Fortunately, the majority of problems are short-lived, but in those cases where they continue to plague us, they often cause major distress.

Impact of sexual difficulties

Most of us can take the occasional sexual hiccup in their stride. Stress, tiredness, illness, and just the normal ups-and-downs of life affect how we behave sexually. Our bodies are not machines and we know that our minds, our hearts, and our souls affect them.

When these hiccups continue for a long period of time they can put an enormous strain on a relationship. Whether it's a problem with low desire or difficulty with arousal or reaching orgasm, it can feel very isolating. We often assume that we are the only ones with sexual problems and too often fall for the myth that sex is natural and therefore should come naturally. We assume that if we're in love, then we won't have any problems making love.

It can be particularly confusing when a sexual problem develops for no identifiable reason especially when, up until then, a couple has enjoyed a great sex life.

If problems are not shared and discussed, resentment builds up. The person with the problem may feel guilty and ashamed that they can't overcome it by themselves and the partner begins to wonder if it's something they've done, or not done. Sometimes fear develops, a fear that if it isn't resolved soon, one or both of them will find someone else.

The reality is that sexual problems are never exclusive to just one person. If your sex life is affected, then both of you have a problem. When couples are able to fully grasp this fact it becomes much easier to work together to overcome it.

Obviously, when problems have a physical cause, your doctor should be able to help. Other problems can be psychological and you may be able to work

through these together. If you find you're not getting over them by yourselves, then consider going to see a psychosexual therapist who will help you work together to get over the difficulty. You can find details of how to get in touch with one in your area at the back of this book.

Another very common set of causes of sexual difficulties are relationship problems. If either of you feels angry or upset with the other, then it is probable that this will affect your sexual relationship. Even if you think you are able to keep your feelings under control, they may still be acted out in the bedroom. If this sounds like you, then you need to sit down with your partner and work through your relationship problems. The sexual difficulties they cause prove that they won't go away on their own. You might want to think about seeing a counselor. Again, details are at the back of this book.

Whatever the cause of the sexual difficulty, I want to reassure you that most couples can and do overcome them. If you can be open and honest with each other, patient and understanding, and share a sense of humor, you can both enjoy a great sex life again.

SEXUAL ABUSE AND TRAUMA

Previous abuse or trauma are very common causes of sexual difficulties. If either you or your partner have had an experience that has left you uncomfortable in any way at all, then you need to talk this through with someone. You might find that talking to your partner or a close friend will help, or you might prefer to talk to someone who is specially trained to help you work through the issues that you've been left with.

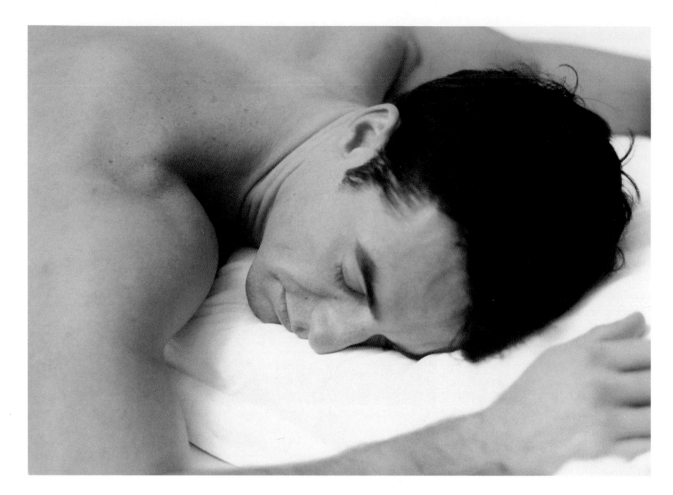

Male problems

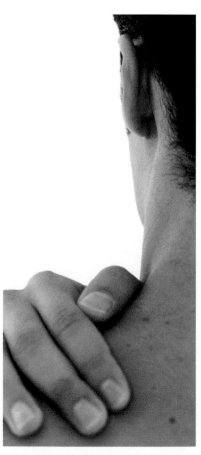

It can be particularly difficult for men to admit to, accept, and talk about sexual problems. The myth of male sexuality says that "real" men are ready for sex 24/7. So if your system crashes, it can be potentially devastating. Here we look at some typical problems and offer some solutions.

Erection problems

Most men will experience erection problems at some stage in their life. In fact it is estimated that up to 40% of men experience problems before they're 40 and 70% by the age of 70. There are a number of medical conditions that can cause erection problems, the most common being diabetes, vascular or heart problems, and neurological disorders. In most cases, psychological factors also play a role.

The most common psychological cause is anxiety. Most men don't have a problem shrugging off the occasional "flop." For others, the experience can be deeply humiliating. Unfortunately, this creates the anxiety that is likely to make the problem reoccur, so many men find themselves in a Catch 22 situation.

Self-help

The best way to cure erection problems is to develop a sense of humor and have a supportive, understanding partner. A woman who sees her partner's occasional erection problem as a reflection on her attractiveness will add additional pressure to an already anxious partner. Other points to remember are:

Relax

It's obvious, but essential. Look back at the stuff on relaxation and stress in Chapter 3.

PC exercises

Exercising your pelvic floor will help to increase blood flow to the genital area making arousal quicker. More info in Chapter 1.

Check your environment

Make sure you are in the mood for sex emotionally and physically. If you have a problem with your

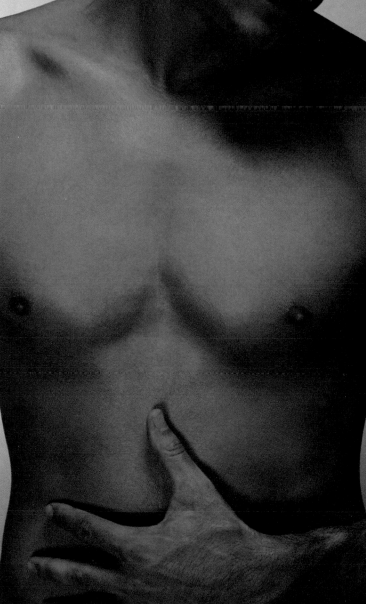

partner, resolve it before you go back in the bedroom.

Use fantasy

Block out anxious thoughts by slipping into a favorite fantasy.

Get sensual

Make sure you take time to enjoy and stimulate all of your body.

In addition to these self-help techniques there are a number of medical choices. Before you start popping Viagra, fully investigate the vacuum pump and pessary options as well as the newer oral drugs, such as Levitra and Cialis.

Premature ejaculation

It's thought that this frustrating condition affects between 30–40% of all males. Men come more quickly in times of stress or after a long time without sex, but when a man has little or no control most of the time, it can cause distress for both partners. Like erection problems, anxiety is known to contribute to fast ejaculation, but the most common reason is that the body becomes conditioned to respond quickly to stimulation. This conditioning is often caused by a speedy masturbation habit. It's also been discovered that some men are born with a highly responsive central nervous system, which makes them quick reactors. Excellent if you are an Indy 500 racing driver, but not so good in the bedroom!

Self-help

Ridding yourself of anxiety is essential, so your first line of attack is stress relief and relaxation. Also, focus fully on your sensations. Contrary to what common sense might tell you, the last thing you should do is think about something else. Conjuring up images of your mother-in-law or counting backward will give you less control, not more. Your goal is to train your body to recognize and tolerate ever-higher levels of sensation and for you to be able to adjust yourself accordingly. To do this you could try:

Exercise your pelvic floor
Many men say they are able to delay ejaculation by "squeezing" or "pushing" their pelvic floor muscles.

DRUG TREATMENTS

Some men have found the SSRI group of anti-depressants very effective at slowing their response time, but there can be other unwanted side effects. A number of new drugs are currently being trialed, and these should become available soon.

Stop and start

This will help you to recognize the point of inevitability. Start by stimulating yourself to the point just before ejaculation, then stop. Start again when the sensations have subsided. Repeat this three times. Gradually you should find the length of time before each stop is getting longer.

Change strokes

When you've gained more control with the stop-and-start technique, try changing your stroke to something less stimulating, rather than stopping altogether. If you're having intercourse, also try changing position.

Delayed or absent ejaculation

This is a much less common problem but one that can be particularly difficult to understand. Suffers from this condition do not conform to the myth that men struggle to control their urges. On the contrary, they find it very difficult, if not impossible, to reach orgasm. Partners often feel inadequate and blame themselves, which can put even more pressure on the man to perform and that just makes matters worse.

If you have problems reaching orgasm on masturbation as well as with a partner, it's worth checking with your doctor that there's no physical cause. Mostly, delayed ejaculation is a psychological problem. While your body may be ready to have sex and you may think you're in the mood, something is blocking you. For some men, it's fear of losing control, for others it's stress and anxiety, for yet others it might be an over concern for their partner.

Self-help

As with all sexual problems, your first line of attack is stress management and relaxation.

Make sure there aren't any lingering problems in your relationship and that you really want to make love to this person. Once that's out of the way:

Be fully present

Ensure you focus on your sensations and are not just waiting for an orgasm. Remember the saying, a watched pot never boils.

Fantasy

Slip into a favorite fantasy to block out negative thoughts and anxieties.

Change strokes

Practice with a variety of sensual and sexual strokes to ensure you're getting maximum stimulation.

Change masturbation routines

Penises can be like creatures of habit, and if you have slipped into the pattern of always masturbating in a certain way, you might struggle to emulate the sensations with your partner. Expand your masturbatory repertoire and gradually your body will learn to respond to a wider variety of touch.

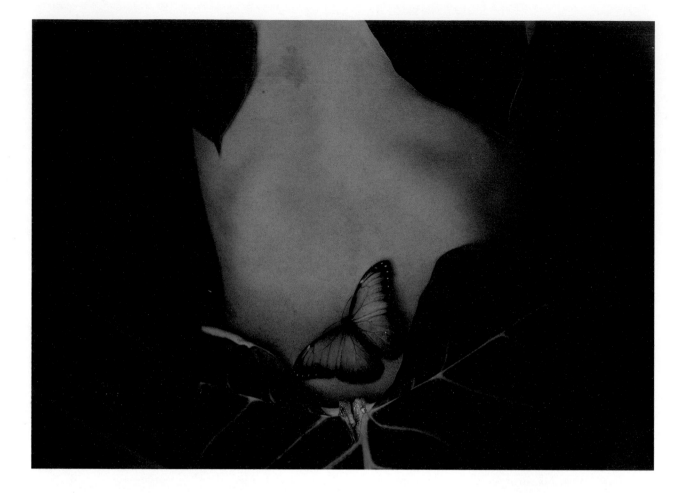

Female problems

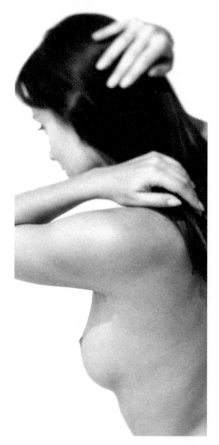

It was once thought that women didn't really enjoy sex, but now the majority of women consider a fulfilling sex life an integral part of their personal wellbeing. Previously, sexual problems were ignored, but now most women are finally liberated enough to want pleasure and satisfaction.

Difficulty reaching orgasm

The most obvious reason for this is lack of adequate stimulation. Some women are able to achieve orgasm alone, but not with their partner, while others are unable to reach orgasm at any time. Some may never have experienced orgasm at all.

Occasionally, there are underlying physical reasons why orgasm may be difficult to achieve, similar to those experienced by men with erection problems. Assuming the women is fully aroused, however, the problem is more likely to be psychological.

Psychological reasons include feeling self-conscious or having low self-esteem, fear of losing control, shame or guilt about sexuality, and being distracted, perhaps by children or housework, and family matters.

Self-help

Learning to relax is most important. Hopefully, you'll find the information in Chapter 2 helpful for that. It's also essential that you're able to communicate with your partner about the kind of stimulation you need. Chapter 4 will give some helpful advice for getting the conversation going. Once that's out of the way, you might find the following orgasm triggers helpful:

• Breathe deeply or pant to pump extra oxygen into tensing muscles.

• Arch your back or try a different position to maximize clitoral stimulation.

• Rhythmically squeeze your pelvic floor muscles.

• Escape into a fantasy to block out any distractions or negative thoughts.

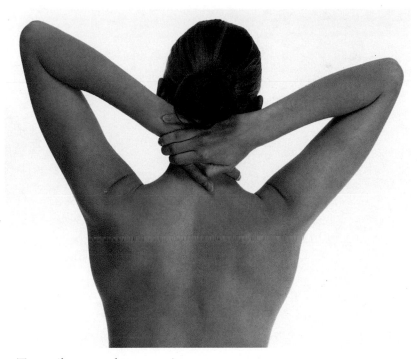

• Try a vibrator—the extra stimulation will strengthen the reflex required to trigger an orgasm.

Painful intercourse

Painful intercourse is common to many women at some stage in their life. Sometimes, it is because of an underlying physical problem such as endometriosis or fibroids, or after childbirth. For the majority of women, however, painful intercourse is due to not being sexually aroused enough. For some women, intercourse is blocked completely because the vaginal muscles go into an involuntary spasm—this condition is known as vaginismus.

Self-help

Many women find that they get caught up in a cycle. Because intercourse has been painful, they fear more pain and become anxious. And because they're anxious, they don't get aroused. And when they're not aroused they'll experience pain again—and so the cycle continues. Breaking this cycle means learning to fully relax and having a supportive partner who is willing to

Recent research suggests that as many as four in every 10 women suffer from sexual problems

do everything they can to maximize arousal. If you still experience pain on intercourse when you know you're fully aroused, then you should check with your doctor to rule out any underlying gynecological problem.

Additional help for vaginismus

Many women find that they can overcome this by very slowly and gradually stretching the vaginal muscles. Start by ensuring your fully relaxed and aroused and then, using plenty of lube, try and insert just the tip of your little finger. As that becomes comfortable, see if you can insert your forefinger. Taking as much time as you wish—and this process can take months so be patient—continue to stretch by putting a finger deeper in, and then perhaps two. When you're ready, practice with your partner's finger. It can take quite some time to recondition the muscles of the pelvic floor, but it can and does happen, so don't lose heart.

Cystitis

This is a very common condition that some women seem to be particularly prone to. The bladder becomes inflamed due to a bacterial infection and the sufferer frequently needs to go to the bathroom and may experience pain on urination. Strictly speaking, it's not a sexual problem, though extended lovemaking will make the condition worse and can trigger an inflammation, hence the expression "honeymoon cystitis."

Self-help

The best treatment is to drink, drink, and drink some more, preferably something alkaline that will neutralize the urine. Cranberry juice or barley water are favorites, and water helps

flush the infection out. If the condition continues a doctor can prescribe antibiotics.

Thrush

This common fungal infection often affects the vagina and vulval area. It is very itchy and sex can be extremely uncomfortable and make the condition worse for the sufferer. It's also possible for men to catch the infection but since the man may have no symptoms he may be inadvertently re- infecting his partner. Like cystitis, it tends to be a recurring condition.

Self-help

Various creams and pessaries are available over the drugstore counter that quickly clear up the condition. Some women also find that going on a yeast-free diet prevents the condition from reoccurring.

Most sexual problems can be significantly improved by learning the art of relaxation

Desire problems

A growing number of people are struggling with sexual addiction while at the other end of the spectrum, many more feel that they have no sexual desire at all. The majority of people fall somewhere between these two extremes. Each person's libido will vary over their lifetime.

We know that sexual desire varies from person to person, and that each person's libido will vary over their lifetime, depending on their relationship and other circumstances in their life.

The fastest growing area seen by psychosexual therapists are problems with desire, or libido as it is sometimes called. One of the most common difficulties that couples have to face is when their sexual appetites are very different.

Managing differences in desire

There is no right number of times that you should have sex in a relationship. If one of you wants sex every day and other is happy with it once in two weeks, you are both normal. There will be times during your relationship when your desires are almost equally matched. For example, in the early days of a relationship when PEA levels are high, both of you are likely to feel very horny indeed and thoroughly enjoy getting close to each other. But when this wears off (usually around 12–18 months later), then sexual desire tends to go back to an individual's natural norm.

We also know that desire changes with age. A man's testosterone is at its peak in the late teens while a woman's is premenopausal. Unfortunately, this mismatch can mean that a couple's desires are sometimes out of synch. The time when couples seem to be most equal is in their fifties.

We also know that a woman's libido changes a lot in the course of the menstrual cycle, so she may want sex every day for a few days a month and then not at all for another two weeks, a fact many men find confusing and frustrating.

If you have different desires, then compromise and negotiation are the solution. Many couples

find they slip into a negative pattern where the partner with the higher libido is regularly asking for sex and being rejected. The person with the lower libido can also slip into the habit of avoiding physical contact unless they're in the mood for sex because they are frightened that it will give off the wrong signals.

It's essential that as a couple you commit to physical intimacy, and that you continue to be affectionate and sensual, regardless of whether or not it leads to sex. Both of you will miss out if the only time you have contact is when you have sex. As a couple, you need to commit to creating a tender, loving environment in which sex may happen.

Once the scene is set, it's more likely that the person with the lower desire will begin to feel aroused. When you feel aroused, desire kicks in. To avoid an automatic expectation of arousal, some couples agree to specify sex-free days. They continue to be

If you have different desires, then compromise and negotiation are the solution

romantic and sensual, but they both know that it's not going to become sexual.

Another thing to consider is whether or not it's acceptable for you as a couple to have sex when just one of you wants it. How would it feel to lend your partner your body for their pleasure, or lend them a hand? Not all sexual encounters have to be mutual. If you're both comfortable with the occasional sexual favor, then this can relieve pressure.

Gone off sex altogether?

Not feeling like sex for a few weeks during times of stress or illness, or perhaps after a bereavement or having a baby, is perfectly normal. But if your desire doesn't seem to be returning, even when the original cause is long gone, the healthiest of relationships can feel strained. There might be powerful feelings of guilt and rejection and both partners may begin to doubt their sexuality and attractiveness.

Going off sex can be particularly disturbing for men. The myth is that men are always desperate for it, so both you and your partner can be left feeling embarrassed and confused.

Losing desire can be a symptom of a physical illness or a side effect of medication. Occasionally it can be the result of low testosterone. It can also be a symptom of another sexual problem. For example, if you're having problems with erections or reaching orgasm, you might lose desire as well. The most common causes are psychological. Low self-esteem, relationship problems, and negative previous experiences are the most common culprits.

If you find things aren't changing you might want to consider talking through the problems with either your partner, a close friend, or a therapist. There are details of where to find a suitably trained therapist at the back of this book.

Sexual addiction

Sexual addiction seems to be a growing problem, particularly since the advent of the internet with its vast range of sexual services, available inexpensively and anonymously. Conservative estimates claim that between 3% and 6% of the population may be affected.

Sexual addiction is defined as any sexual activity that feels "out of control." The activity might be compulsive masturbation, looking at pornography, sex with a partner, sex with strangers, etc. What makes it an addiction is the fact that the person feels compelled to seek out and engage in their chosen sexual behavior, in spite of the problems it may cause in their personal, social, and working lives.

When we have sex, our bodies release a powerful cocktail of chemicals that make us feel good. An addict becomes driven to seek out this sexual high and, like other chemical addictions, the more they use it, the more they need to relive the same high. In between the highs are the lows, the feelings of regret, shame, and anxiety. The best way to escape the lows is to engage in the activity, so that sex becomes a pain-reliever and the cycle starts all over again.

If you think that either you or your partner may be engaging in sexual activity that feels out of control, then the first step is to

It's essential that, as a couple, you commit to physical intimacy, whether or not this leads to sex

acknowledge that it is a problem. Most addicts can't give up on their own. They will probably have tried on many occasions and failed. A professional therapist may help them to understand what is happening and encourage them to take steps to change to a healthier sexual lifestyle.

Sexual infections

There are currently 25 main sexually transmitted infections, including chlamydia, genital herpes, genital warts, gonorrhea, pubic lice, HIV, scabies, and syphilis. You can contract any one of them—or, if you're really unlucky, more than one—by sleeping with someone just once.

The most prevalent STIs are:

Chlamydia

The most common sexually transmitted infection amongst young people. It is particularly dangerous, since there are very few symptoms and untreated it can cause infertility. It is easily treatable with antibiotics.

Genital herpes

Facial herpes is called a cold sore but you can contract it on the genitals or anywhere else. There is no known cure for herpes though there are treatments available that will help some people.

Genital warts

These are more common than you think and are the same as warts anywhere else on the body. They're easily eradicated but once you get the wart virus, it can take months or even years to completely clear it out of your system, so it often reoccurs.

Gonorrhea

Otherwise known as "the clap," gonorrhea is very common and if left untreated it can cause serious health problems. It is treatable with antibiotics.

HIV

Probably the most frightening and well known STI as it can develop into AIDS. Drugs are being discovered each day to help combat the virus but it can still have very serious, long-term and even fatal repercussions.

Hepatitis B & C

These affect the liver and, though they're easier to catch than HIV, they don't seem to be as well known. Limited treatments are currently available; both forms can cause permanent liver disease.

Pubic lice

Sometimes referred to as "crabs," these tiny creatures live in the pubic hair. They cause itching and bleeding, but can easily be eradicated.

Syphilis

Difficult to detect in the early stages but as it develops can lead to serious problems. It can be easily treated with antibiotics.

Scabies

This is an itchy rash that can appear anywhere on the body. It is caused by a female mite laying her eggs beneath the skin surface. When found, it is easily treated with a special shampoo or lotion.

The most common symptoms of an STI are:

• Unusual discharge or liquid from the vagina or penis.

• Pain or burning when you pass urine.

• Itches, rashes, lumps, or blisters around the genitals or anus

• Pain and/or bleeding during sex.

• Bleeding after sex and/or between periods.

Most STIs, if detected soon enough, can be treated and cured with a simple course of antibiotics. If you have any concern at all that you may have contracted an infection, or have put yourself at risk of catching one, then check with your doctor, family planning clinic, or local Genitourinary Medicine (GUM) clinic. All these services are fully confidential, and if you go to a GUM clinic, your family doctor doesn't have to know about it.

As I have already said, prevention is definitely the best medicine. If you're not in a monogamous relationship and are not sure about the sexual health and habits of your partner, always use a condom.

Helping agencies

A crucial element of a healthy sex life is the ability to draw on the advice and experience of experts, who can help guide you through the complexities of desire, emotion, partnership, and physical love. In this more enlightened age, many authorities are able to offer guidance on everything from rape to personal relationships and women's health.

American Academy of Child & Adolescent Psychiatry (AACP)
Phone: (202) 966 7300
www.aacap.org
Assisting parents and families in understanding developmental, behavioral, emotional, and mental disorders affecting children and adolescents.

American Association for Marriage and Family Therapy (AAMFT)
Tel: (703) 838 9808
www.aamft.org
Counseling services for adults with relationship and sexual problems. The website contains a therapist locator for the whole of the U.S. and Canada.

American Association of Sex Education Counselors and Therapists (AASECT)
Phone: (804) 752 0026
www.assect.org
A national organization that can tell you where to find counselors and therapists in your area who are trained in relationship and sexual therapy.

National Family Planning & Reproductive Health Association
Phone: (202) 203 3114
www.nfprha.org
Provide access to voluntary, confidential, comprehensive, culturally sensitive family planning and reproductive health care services and to support reproductive freedom for all.

The Harry Benjamin Gender Dysphoria Association
Phone: (612) 624 9397
www.hbigda.org
Advice and information on gender and sexual orientation.

American Association on Health and Disability
Phone: (301) 545 6140
www.aahd.us
Advice and help on sexual relationships for the disabled.

Lesbian and Gay Switchboard
PO Box 7324, London N1 9QS, UK

Phone: +44 20 7 837 7324
Information and advice on being gay, lesbian, and bisexual wherever you live in the world.

Men's Health Forum
www.malehealth.co.uk
Men's Health Center
www.coolnurse.com/male_health.htm
Two highly rated men's health information centers on the web.

Teen Hotlines
www.myjellybean.com/life/hotlines.html
Information and advice on sex and relationships for young people in the U.S., Canada, Australia, and the United Kingdom

Rape Abuse and Incest National Network (RAINN)
Hotline: (800) 656 HOPE
www.rainn.org
Confidential information and advice for rape and sexual abuse and details of your nearest rape crisis counseling center.

The American Board of Sexology (ABS)
Phone: (047) 645 1641
www.sexologist.org
Confidential information and advice on finding a sex therapist throughout the United States.

The Helpline USA, Inc.
Phone: (561) 659 6900
www.thehelpline.net
A helpline for all victims of rape or assault as well as other problems, including those that are marriage-related.

The Vulval Pain Society
www.vul-pain.dircon.co.uk
Information and advice for women suffering with vulval pain disorders.

American Social Health Association (ASHA)
Phone: (919) 361 8400
www.ashastd.org
Dedicated to improving the health of individuals families and communities, with a focus on preventing sexually transmitted diseases.

The final word

No matter how many books you read or how much guidance and advice you consume, it is impossible to enjoy great sex all of the time. Our sex lives are influenced by so many factors that are beyond our control. All we can do is commit to giving sex our best shot.

I sincerely hope that reading this book has given you the incentive and information you need to make sex as good as it can possibly be. If you continue to keep your body in optimum condition, work on maintaining intimacy within your relationships, and remain ready to try new things, I firmly believe that you will enjoy great sex for many, many years to come.

Paula Hall
Author